My colorful world

Coloring fun with basic colors

A coloring book for learning about colors

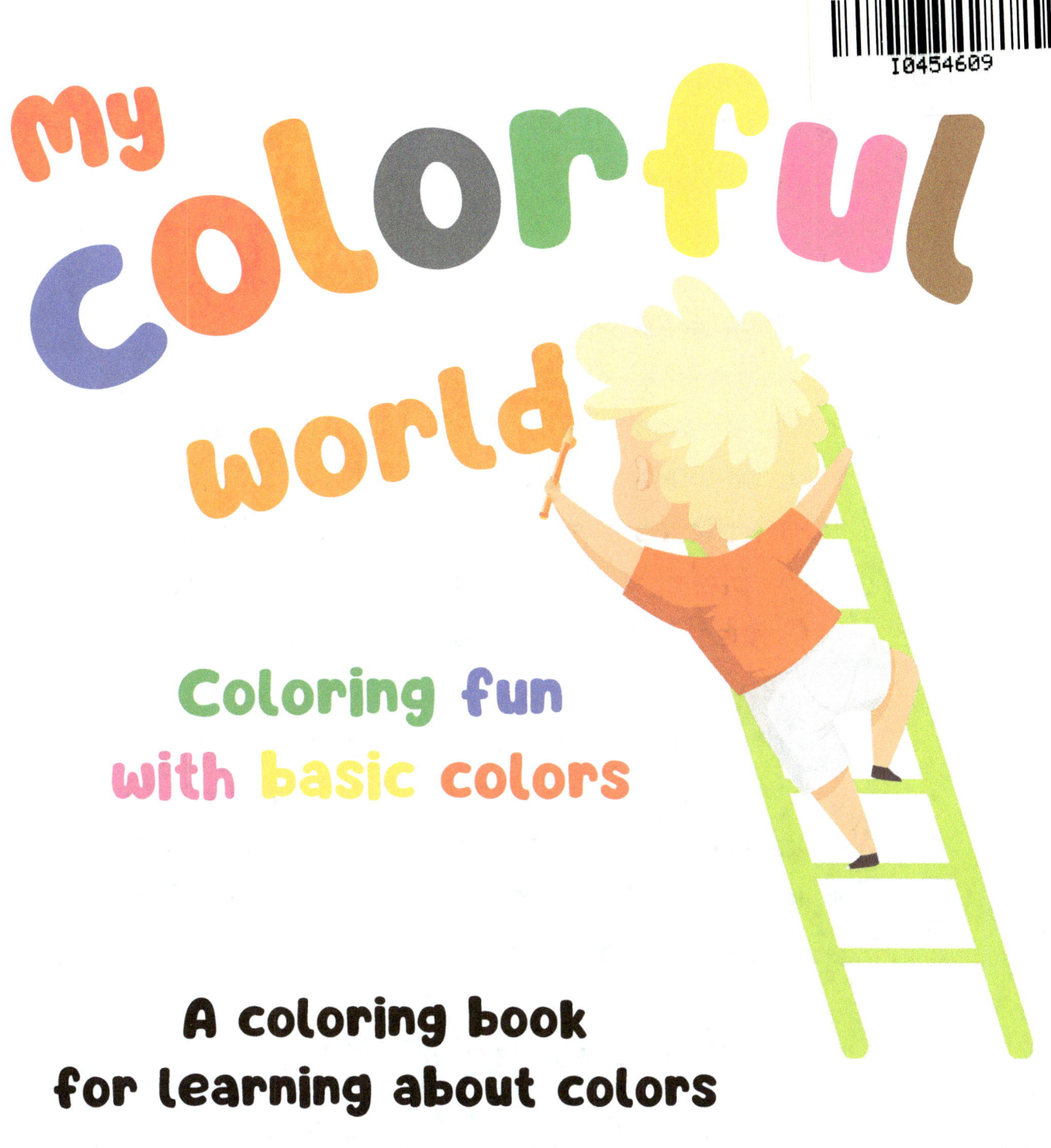

Thank you for choosing

"My colorful world"

Welcome to the enchanting world of colors!

This coloring book introduces fundamental colors
and encourages children to experiment
with the colors in their surroundings.
Young explorers will enjoy exploring different
hues in their daily environment.

Children will improve their understanding
of colors by coloring the pages.
We believe that this book will be a fun way
for kids and their grown-ups to spend time
together as they color and talk.

Have a colorful time!

This book belongs to

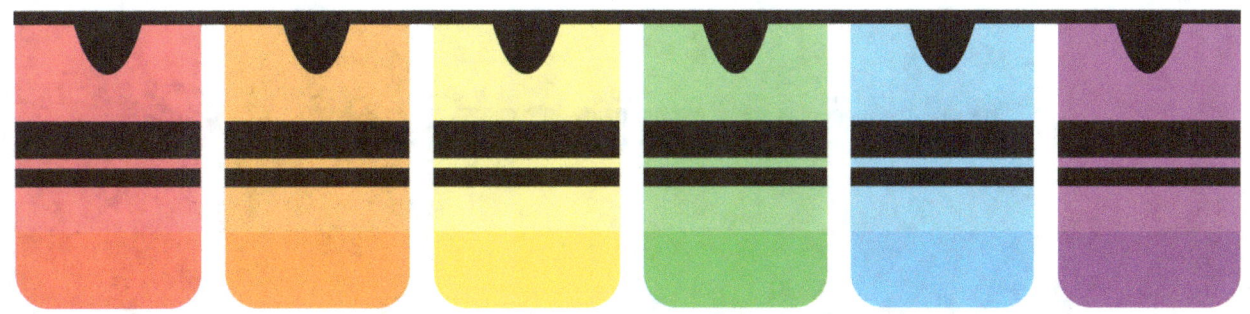

What color is this?

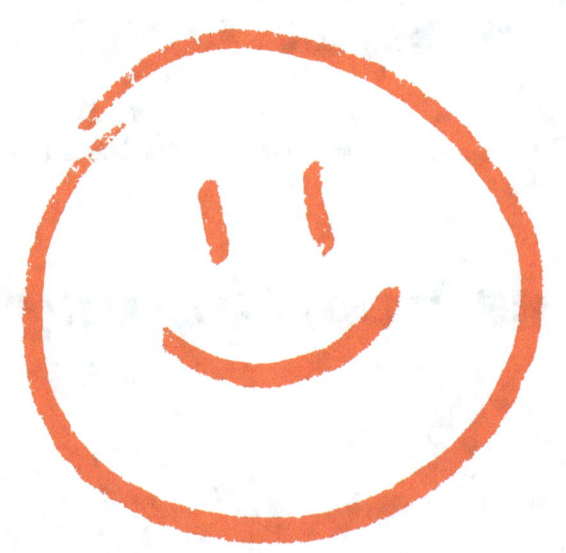

This is Red

What is something Red?

Let's color them!

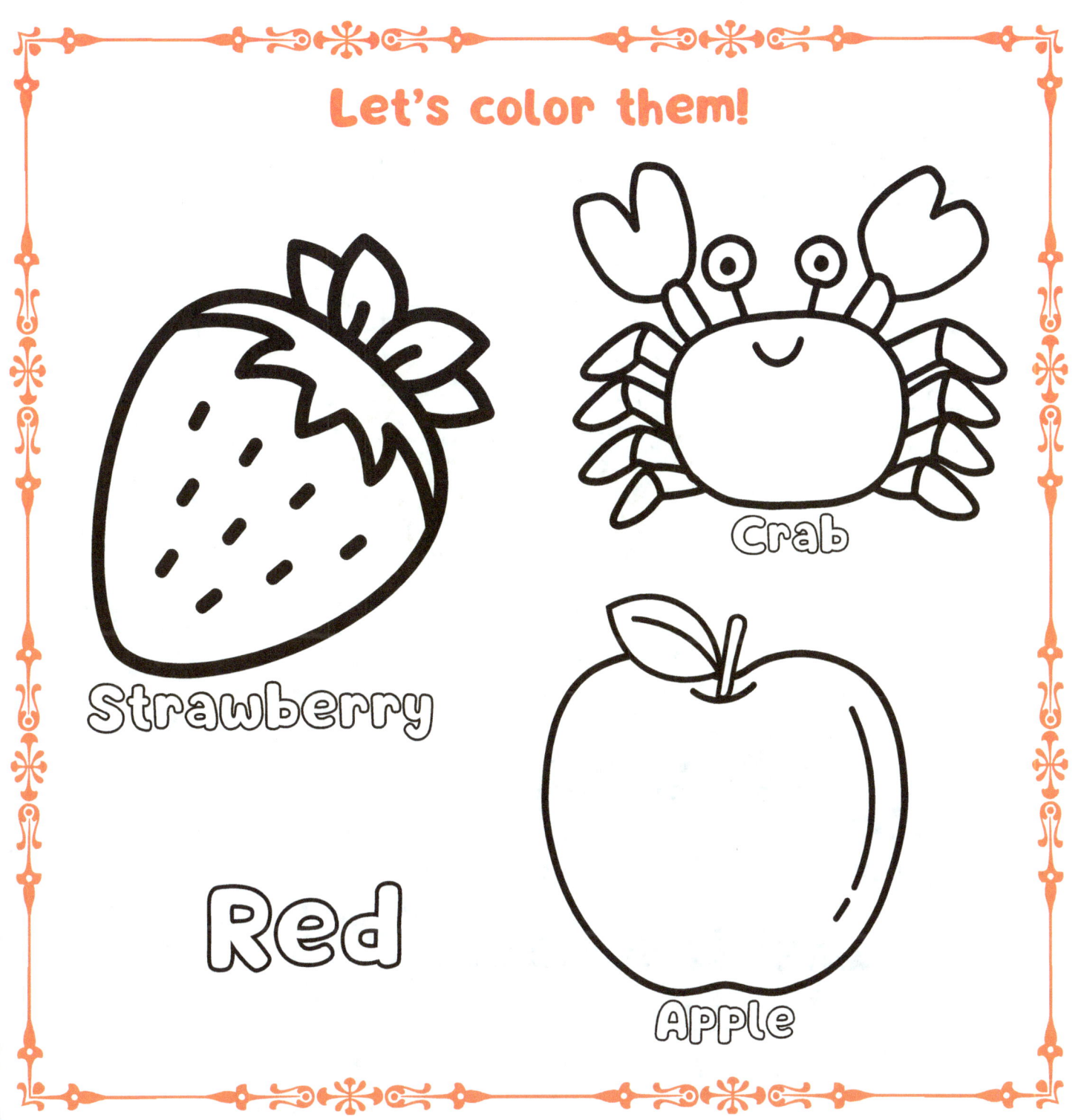

Strawberry

Crab

Red

Apple

What color is this?

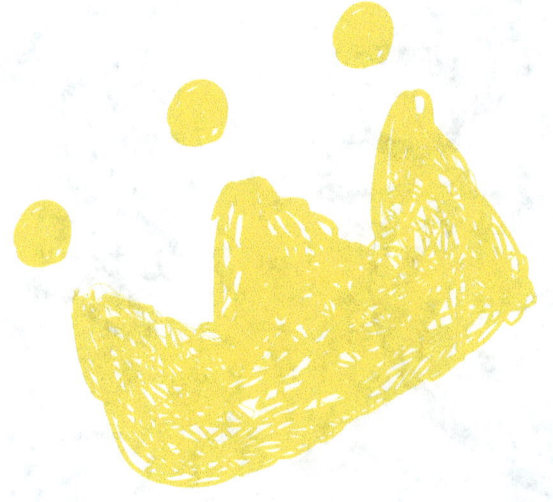

This is Yellow

What is something Yellow?

Let's color them!

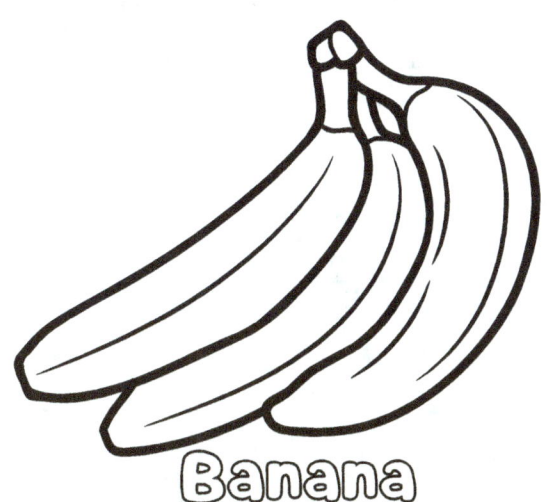

Banana

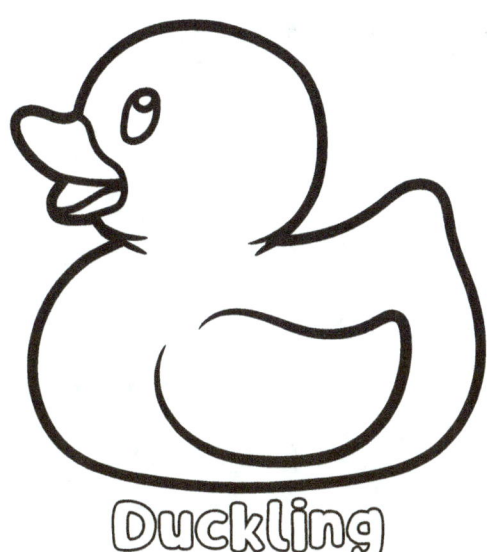

Duckling

Yellow

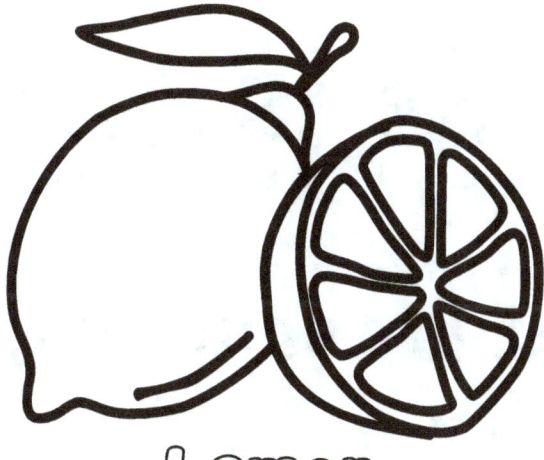

Lemon

What color is this?

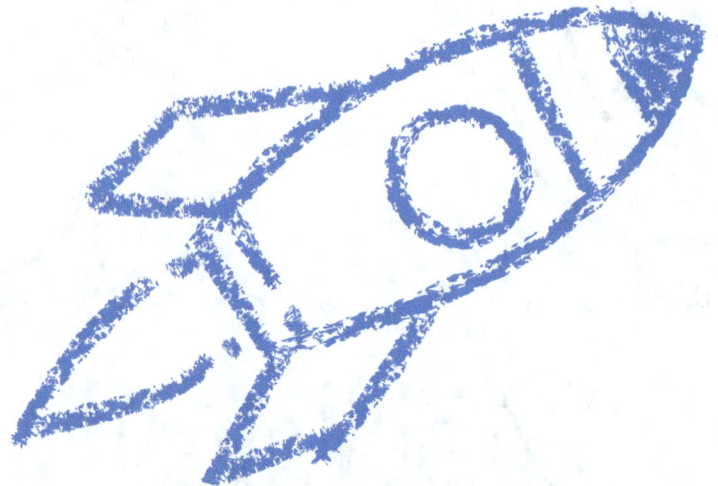

This is Blue

What is something Blue?

Let's color them!

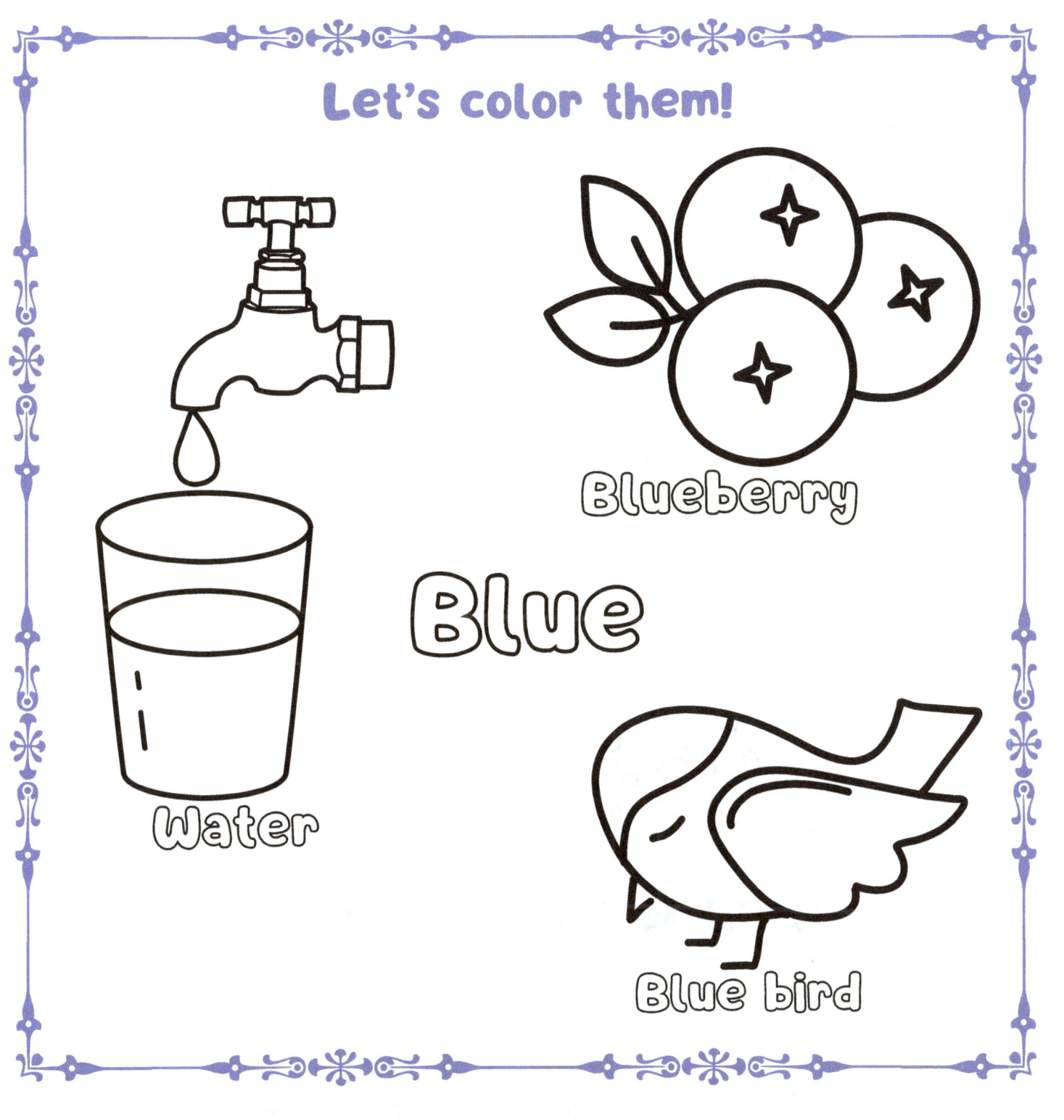

Blueberry

Blue

Water

Blue bird

What color is this?

This is Pink

What is something Pink?

Let's color them!

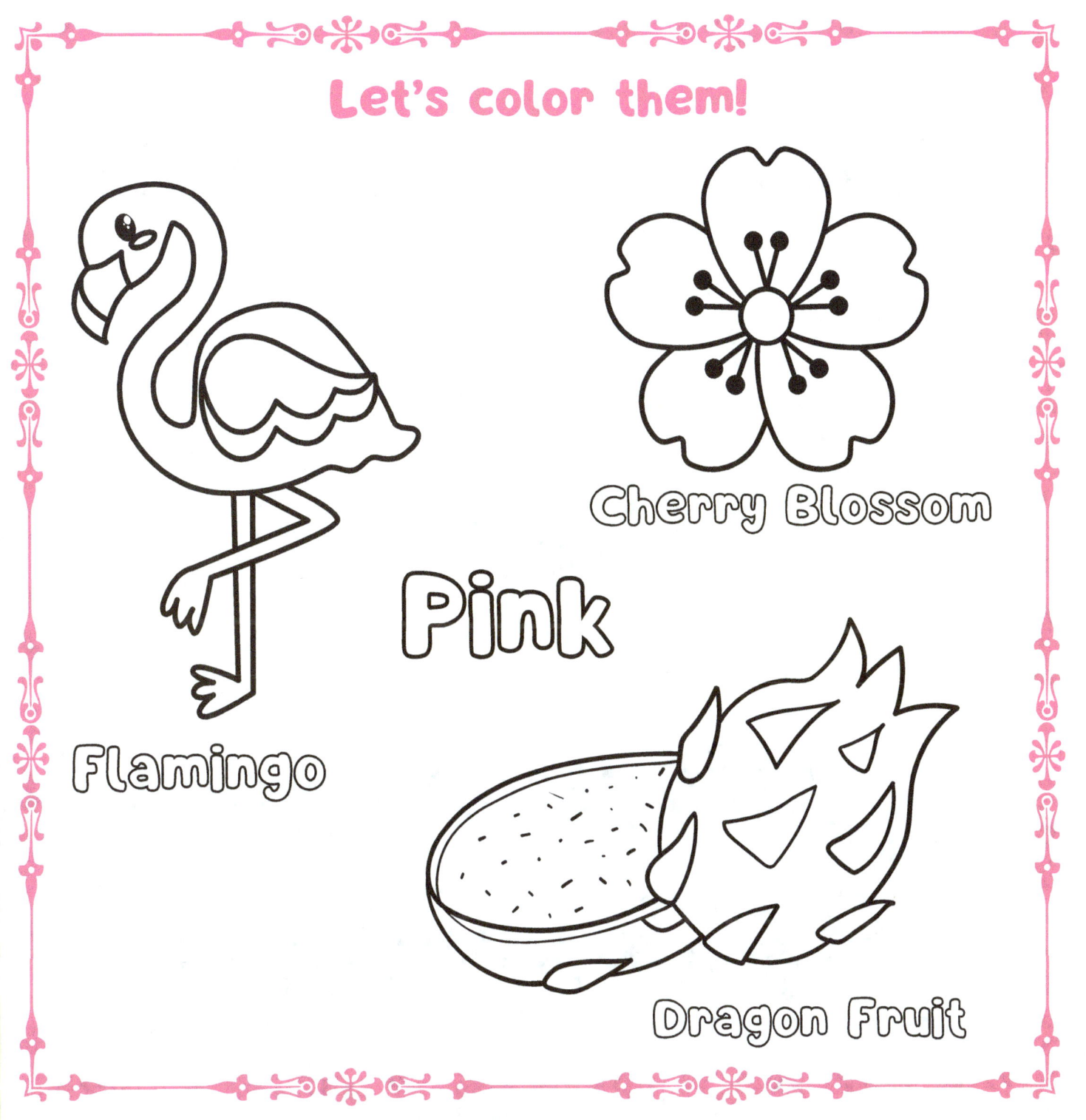

Cherry Blossom

Pink

Flamingo

Dragon Fruit

What color is this?

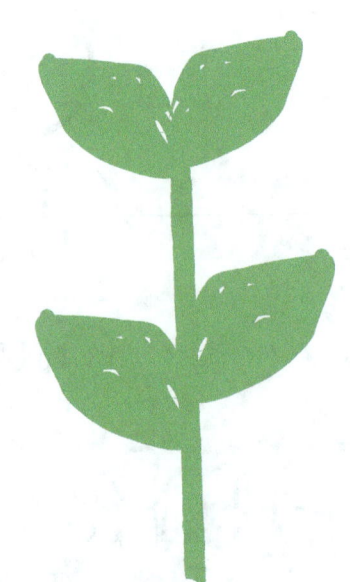

This is Green

What is something Green?

Let's color them!

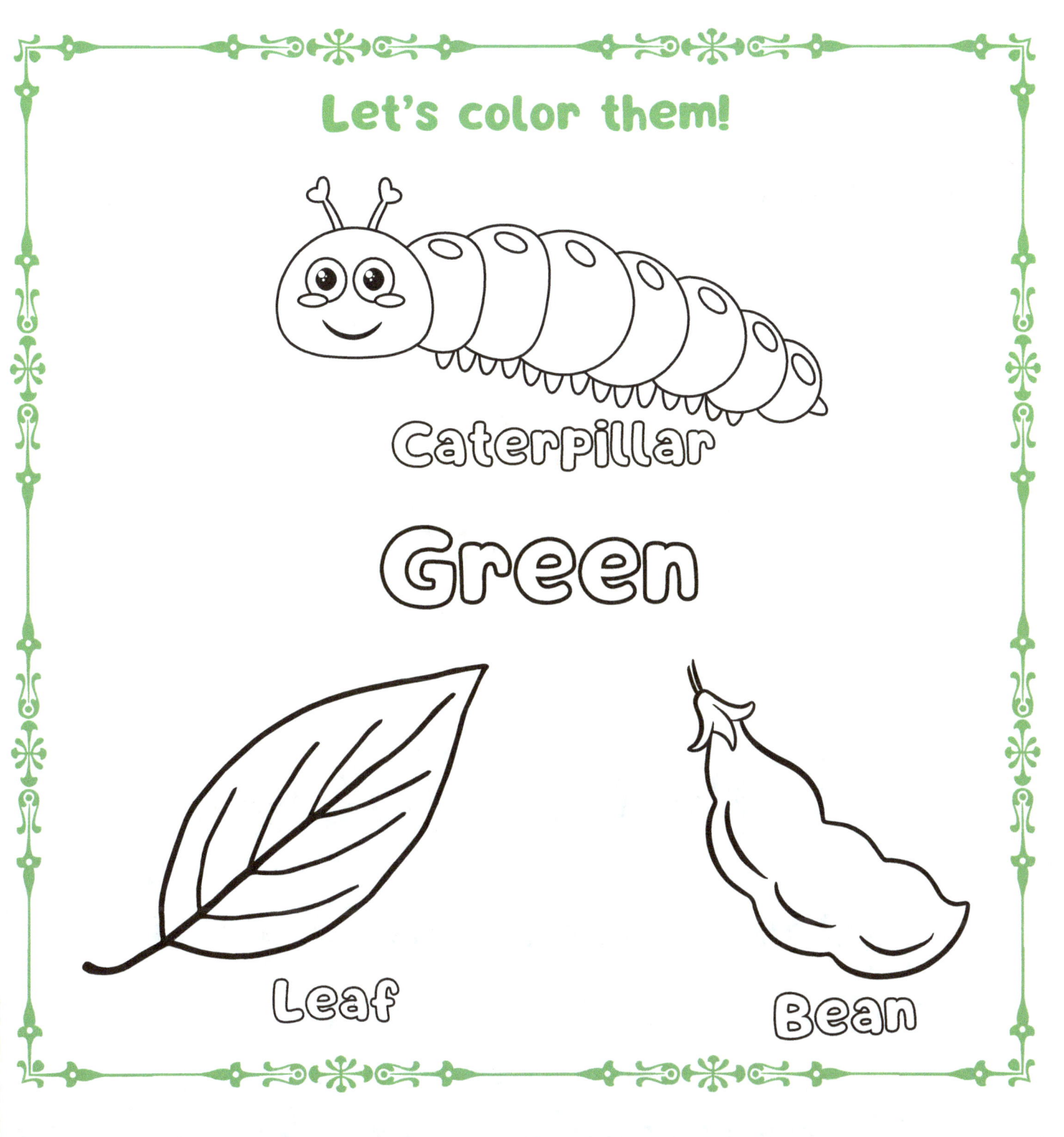

Caterpillar

Green

Leaf

Bean

What color is this?

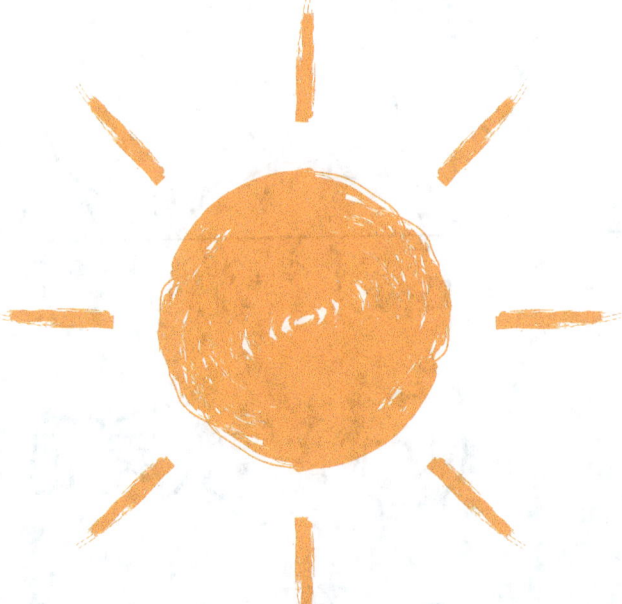

This is Orange

What is something Orange?

Let's color them!

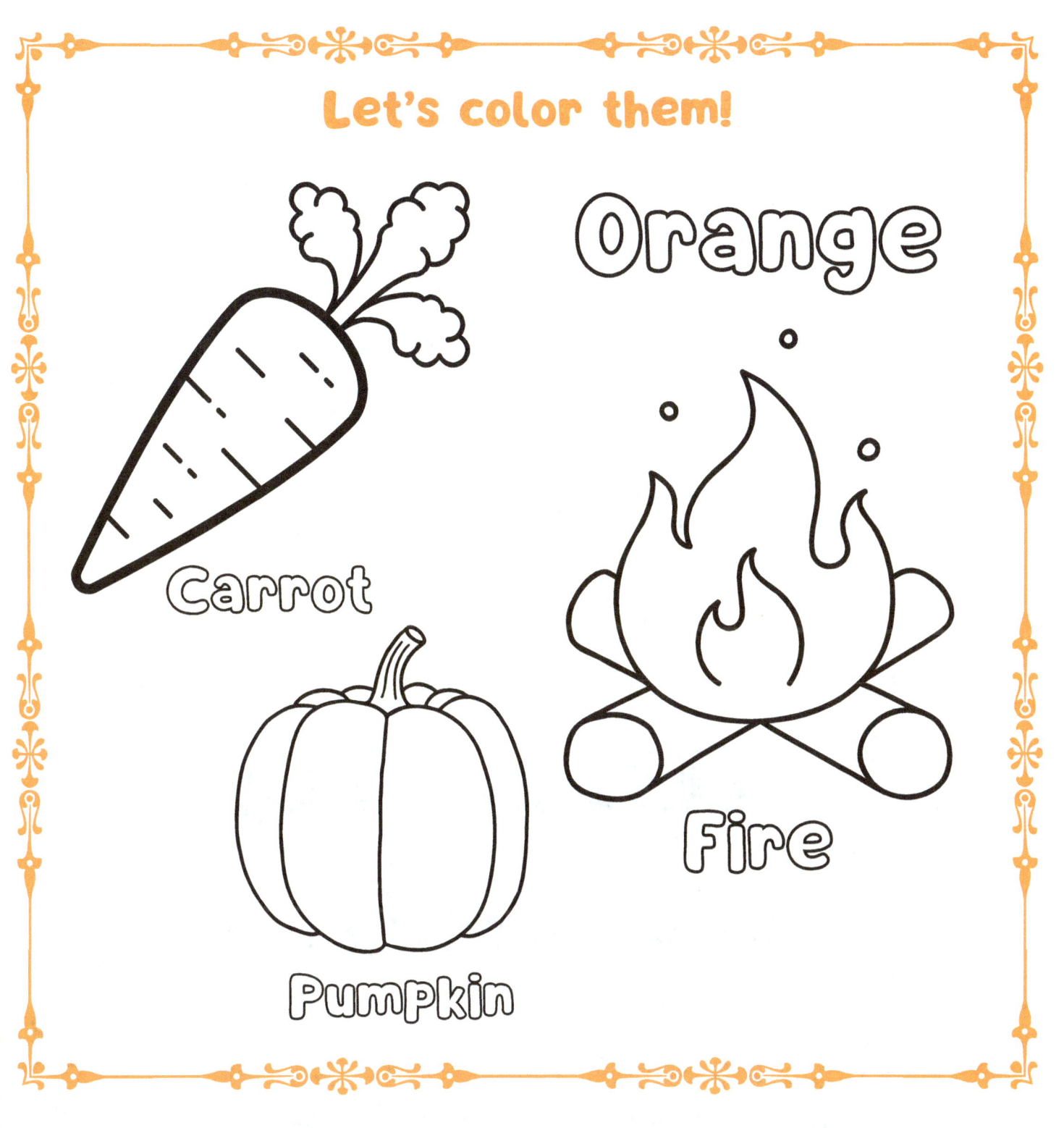

Carrot

Orange

Pumpkin

Fire

What color is this?

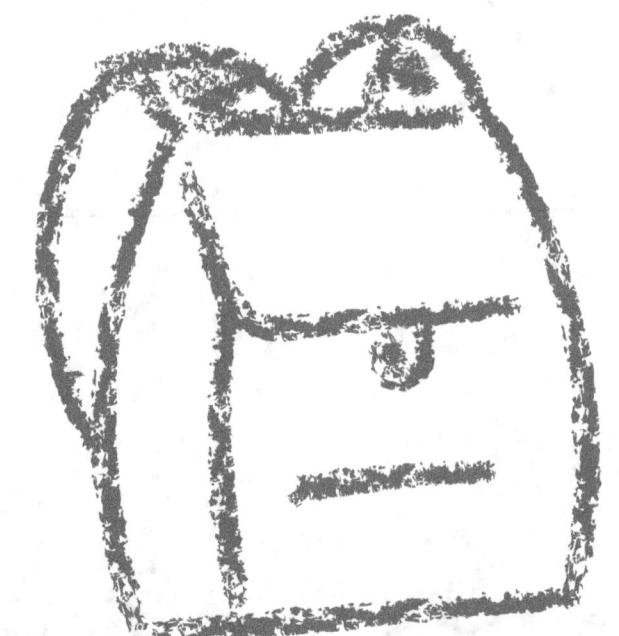

This is Gray

What is something Gray?

Let's color them!

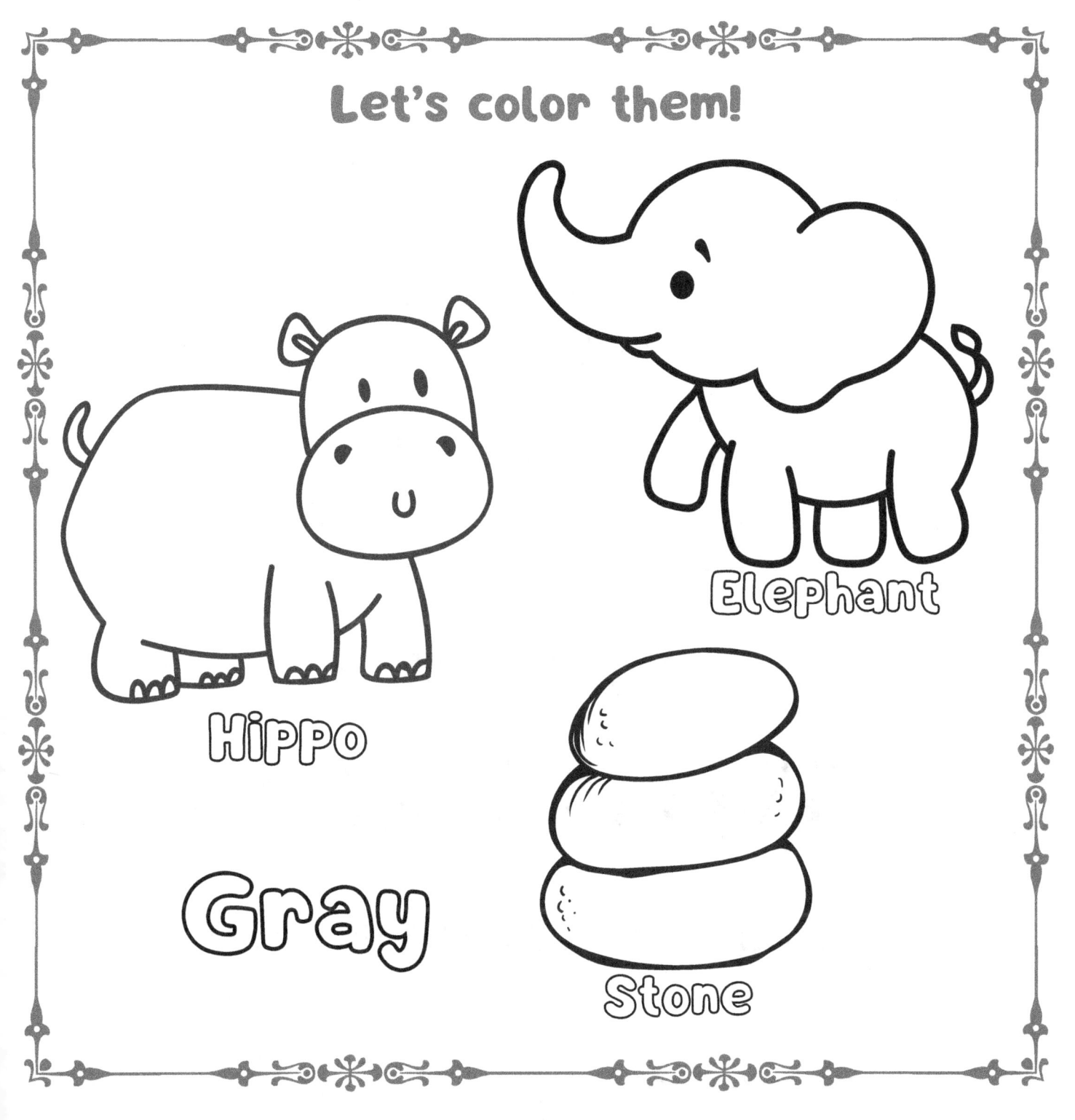

Hippo

Elephant

Gray

Stone

What color is this?

This is Purple

What is something Purple?

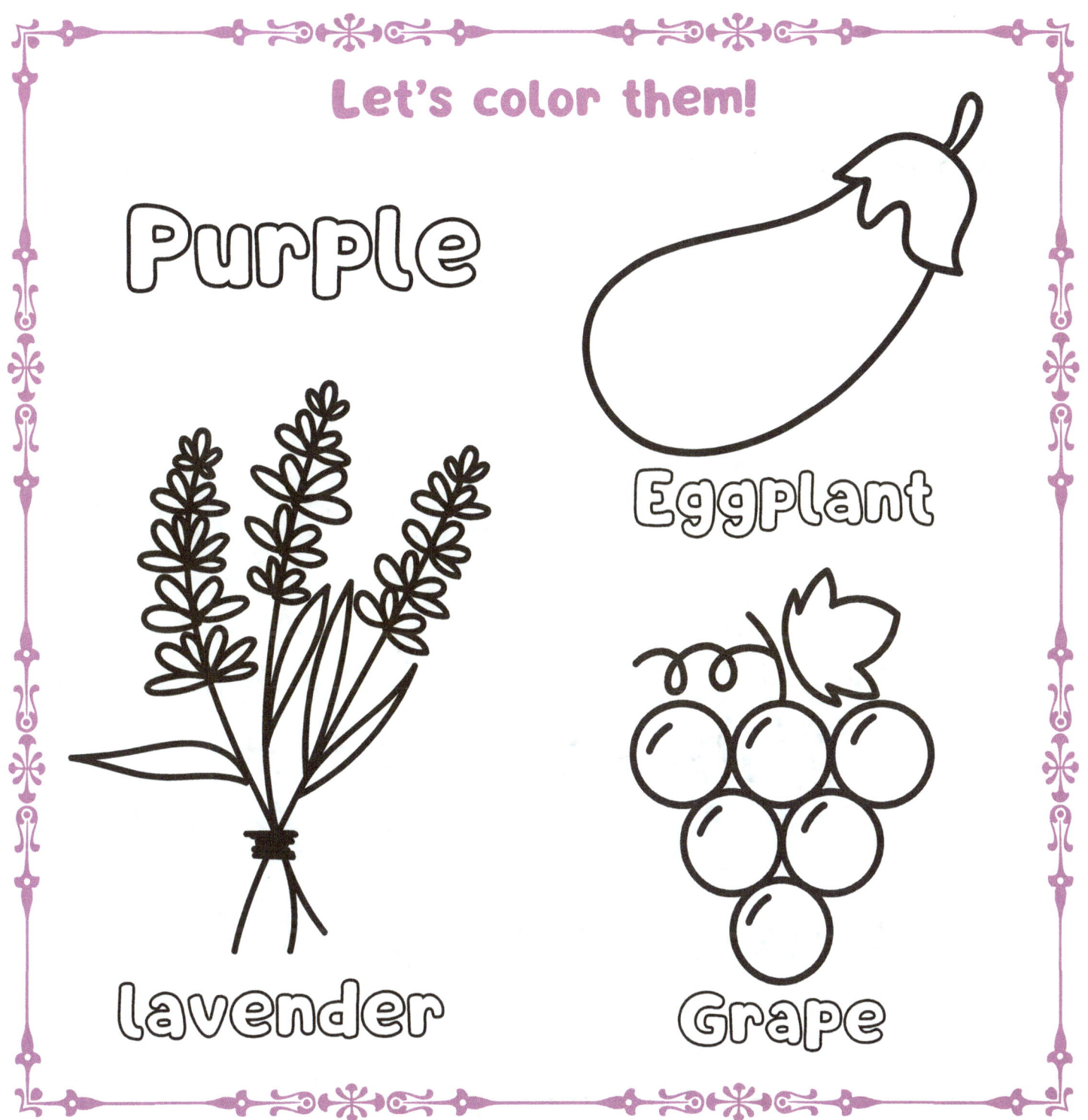

What color is this?

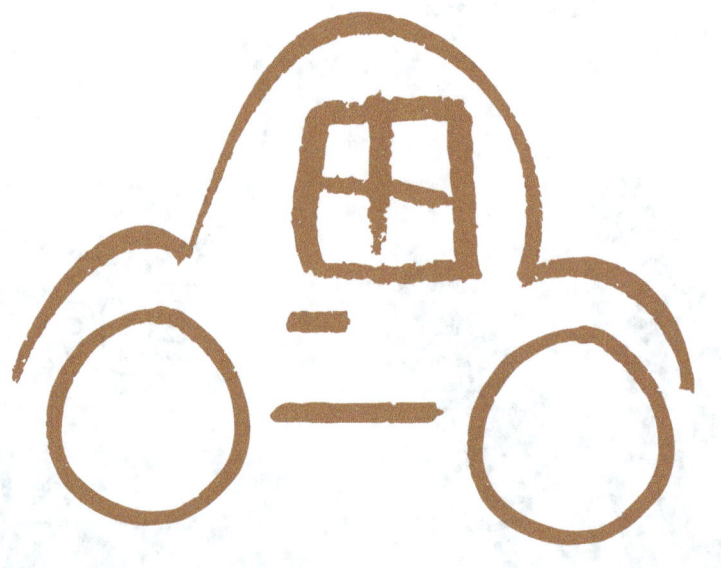

This is Brown

What is something Brown?

Let's color them!

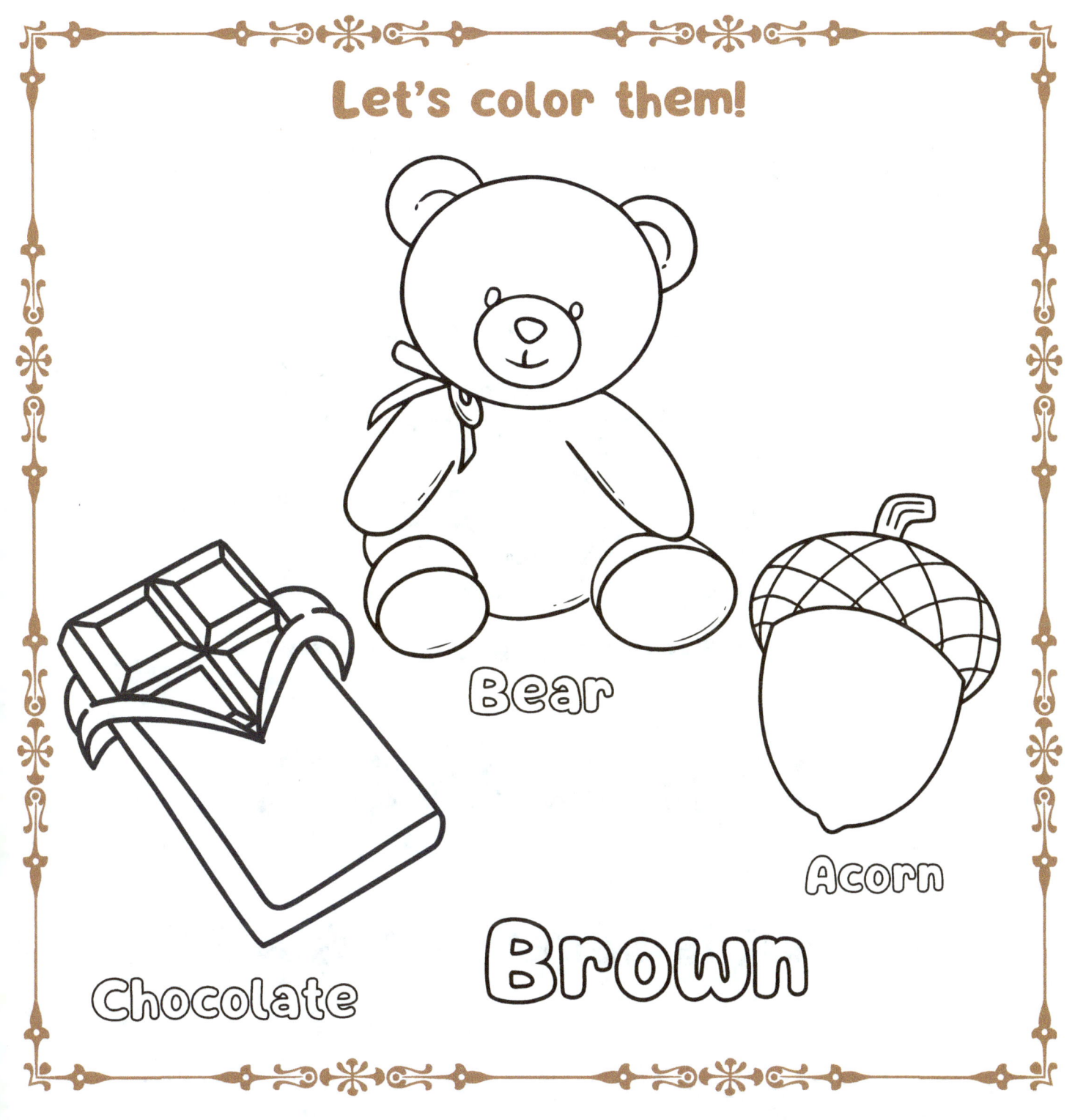

Bear

Acorn

Chocolate

Brown

What color is this?

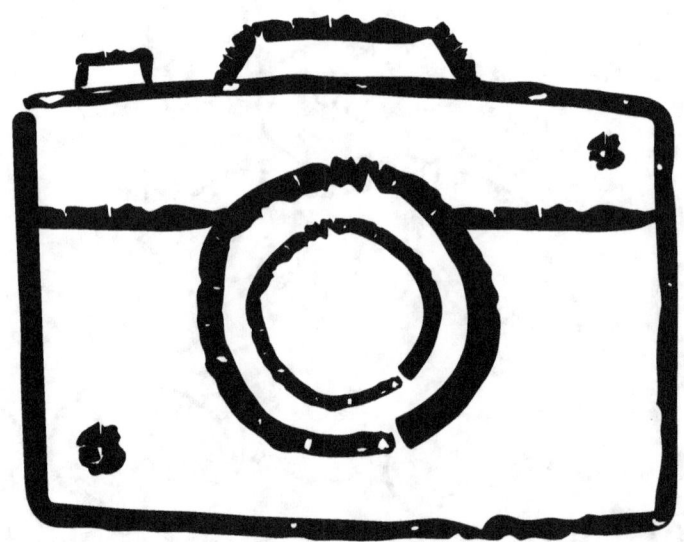

This is Black

What is something Black?

Let's color them!

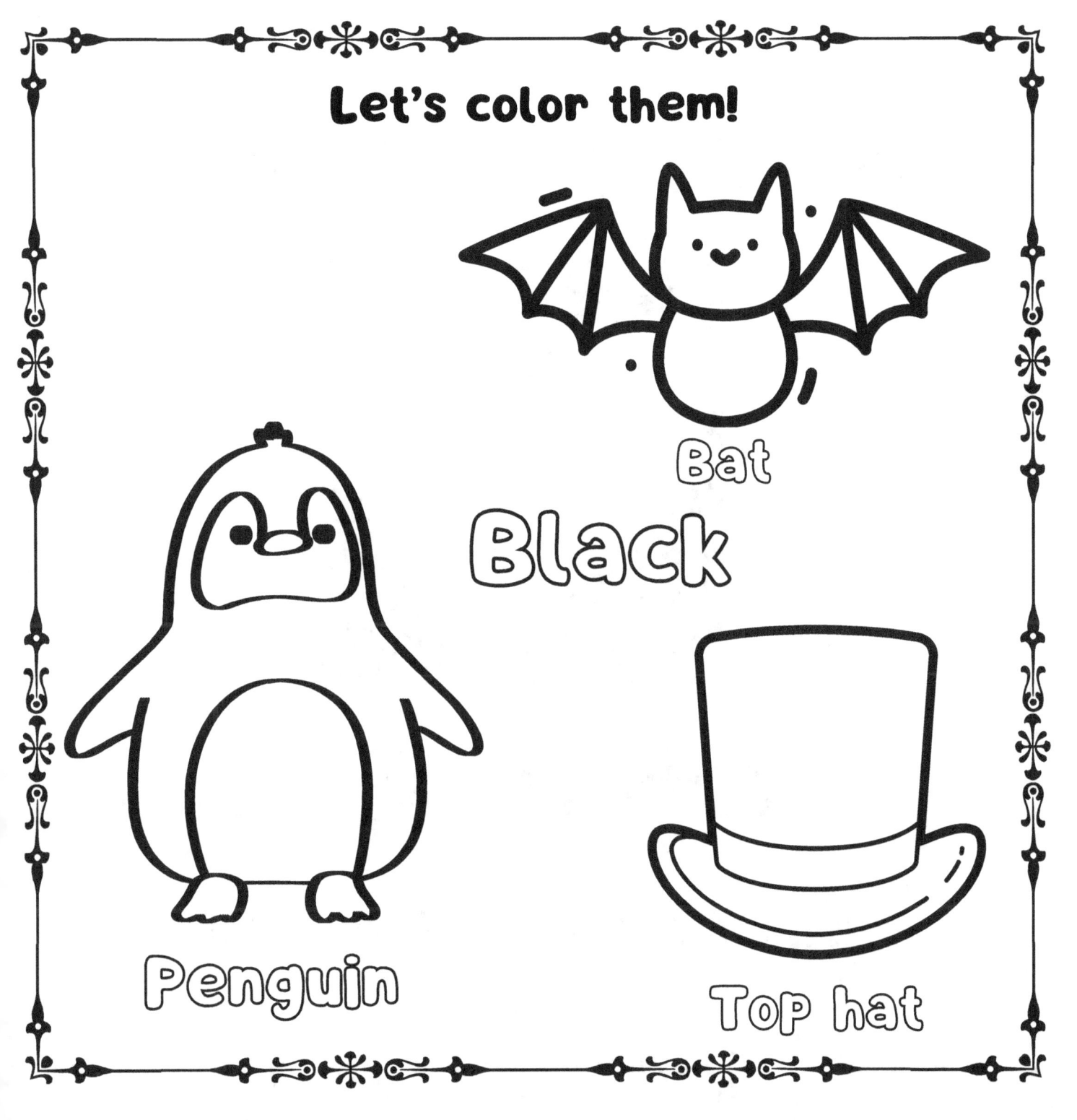

Bat

Black

Penguin

Top hat

What color is this?

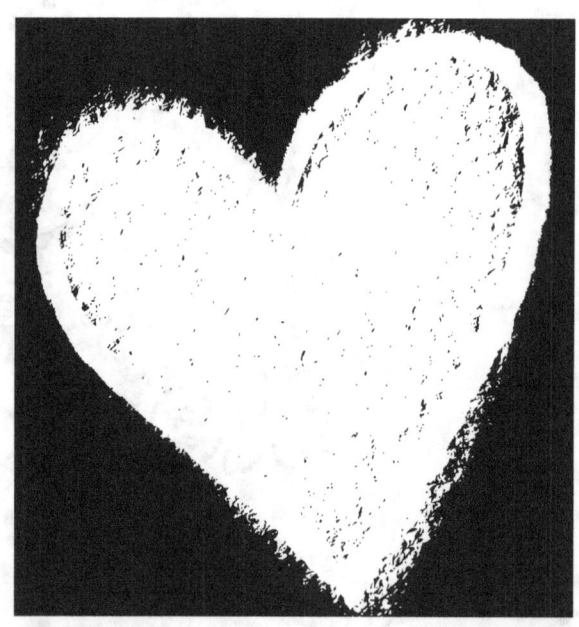

This is White

What is something White?

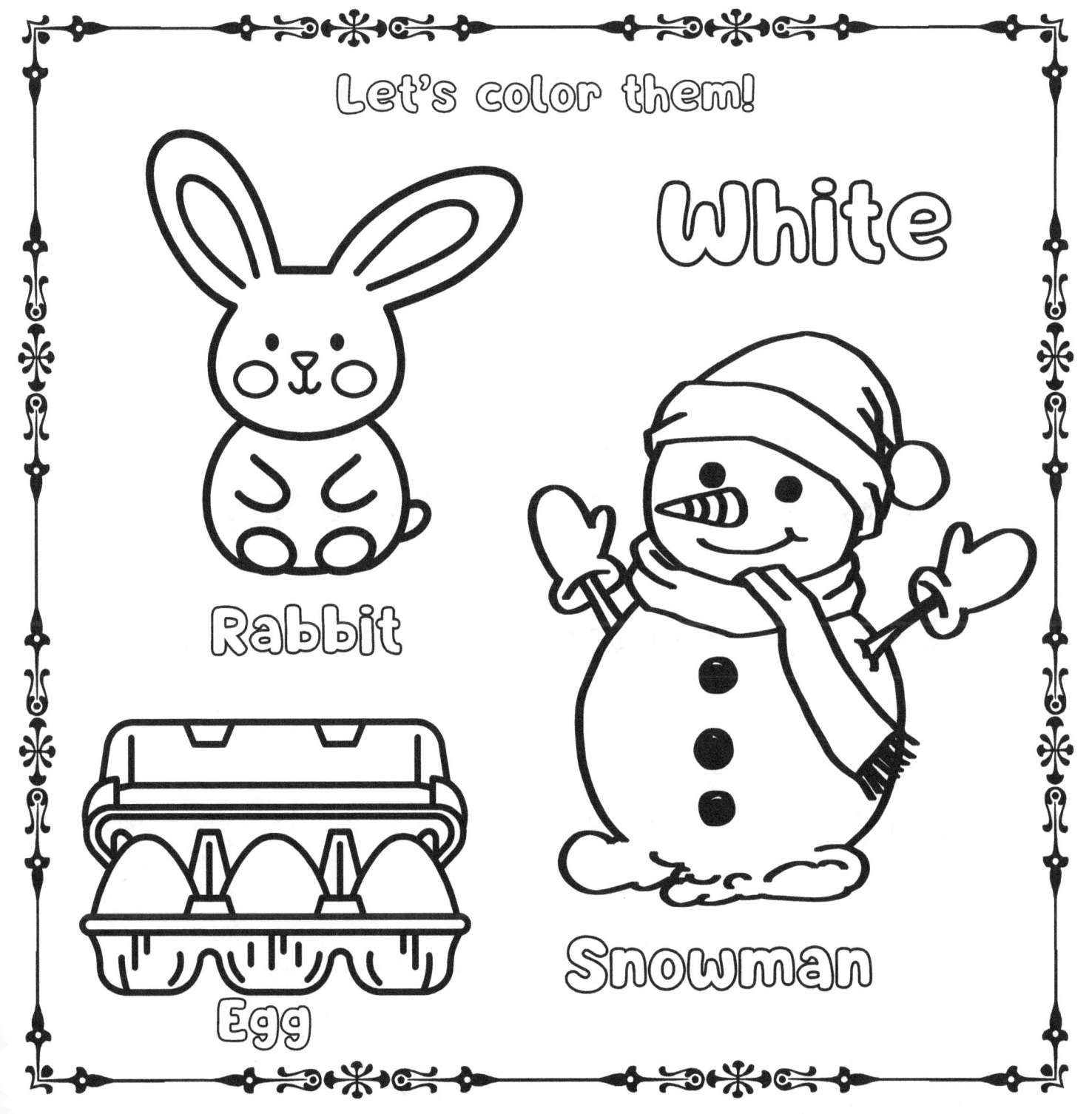

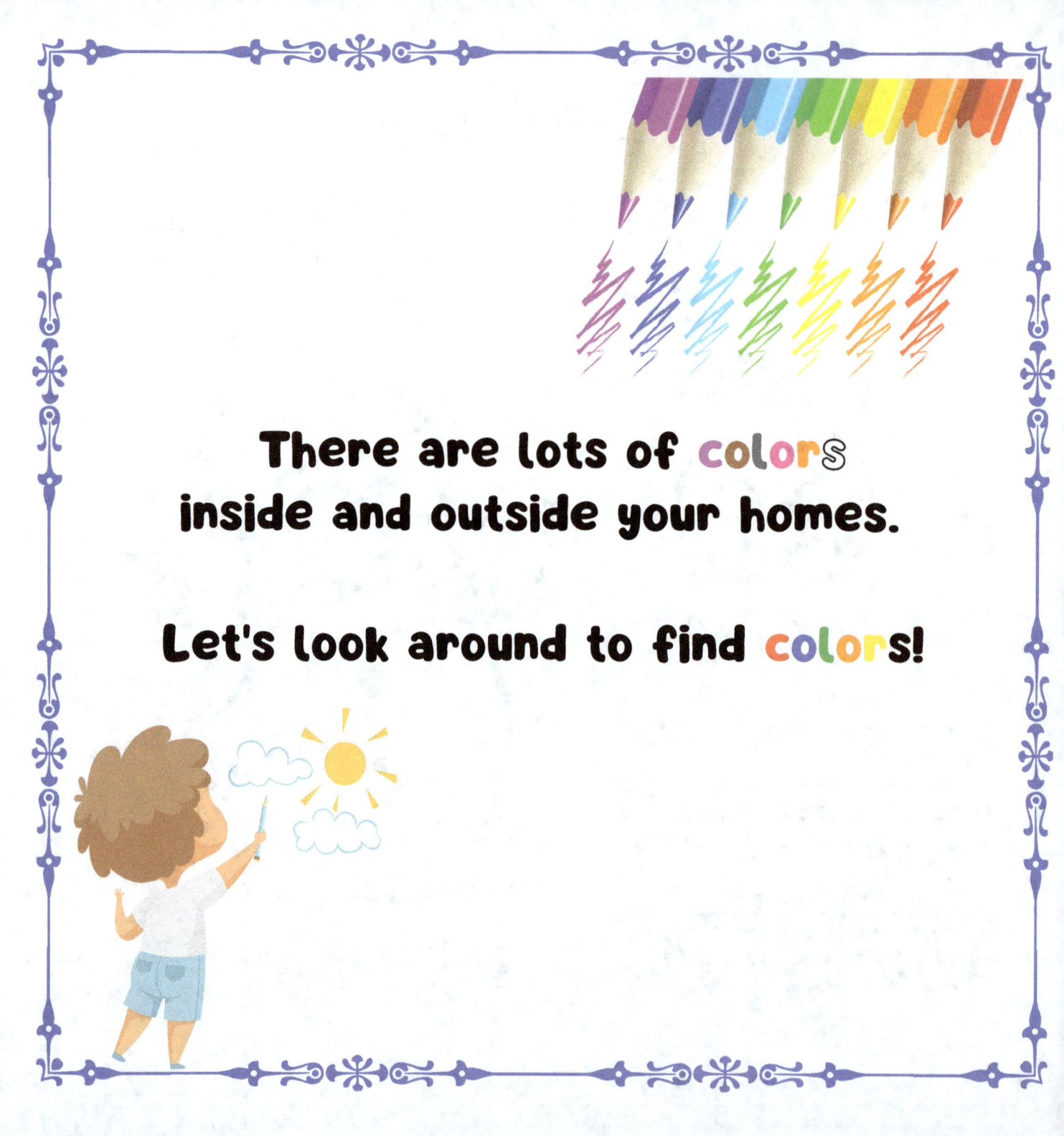

There are lots of colors
inside and outside your homes.

Let's look around to find colors!

What colors can you find?

Let's use different colors to color things.

If you find something new,
ask a grown-up

You can also use your chosen
colors for these!

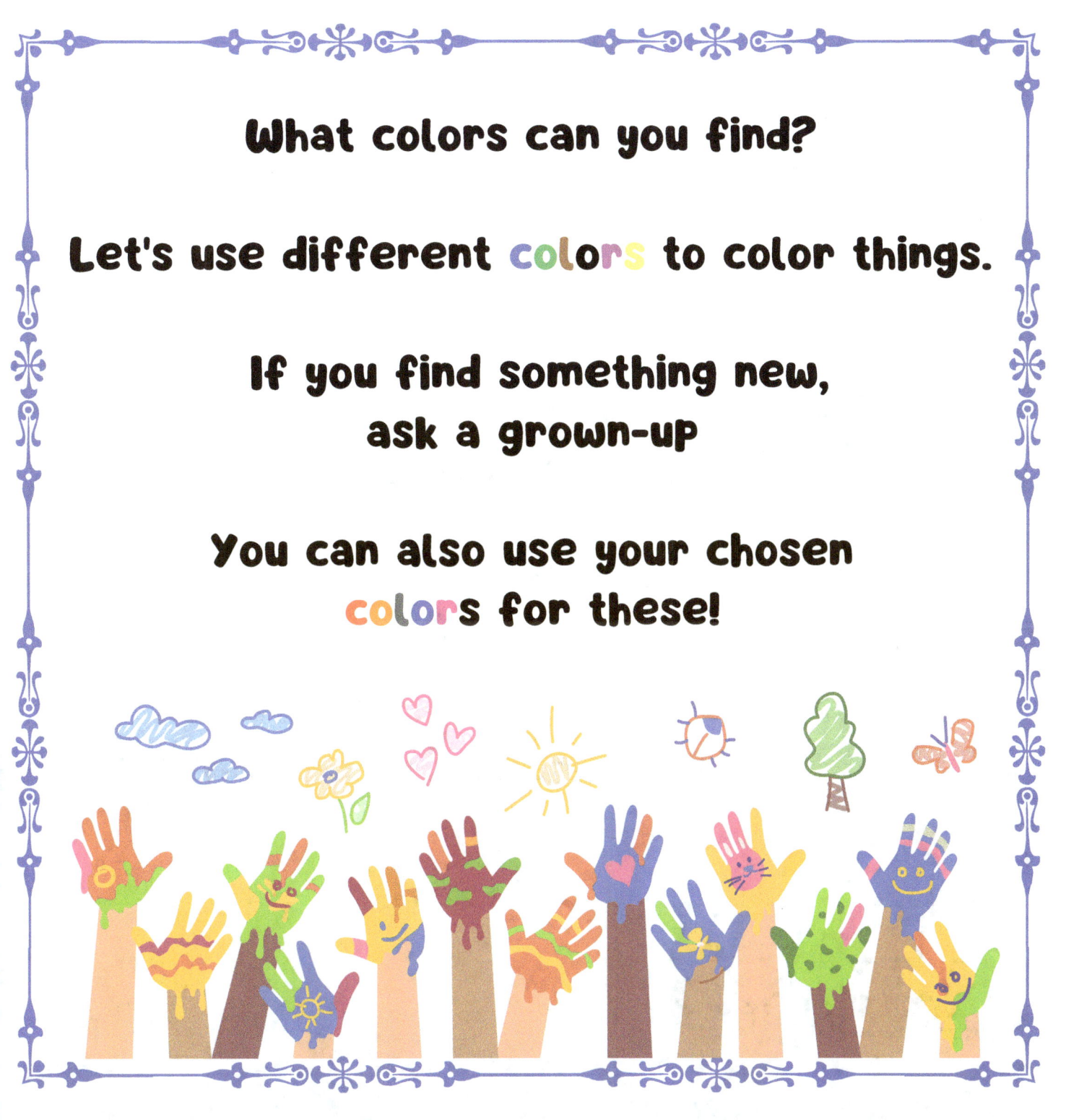

What colors can you find?

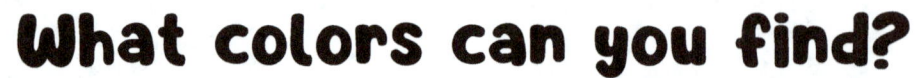

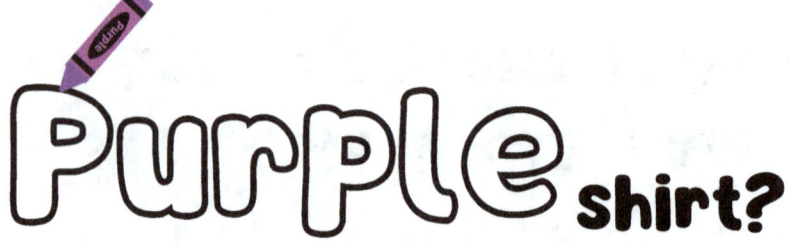 **Purple** shirt?

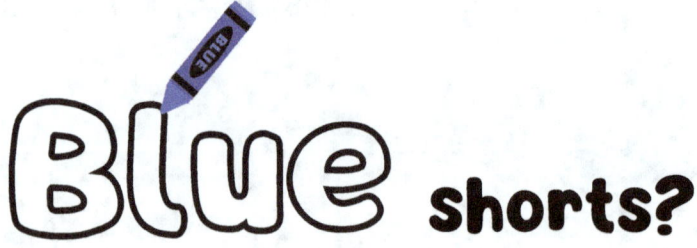 **Blue** shorts?

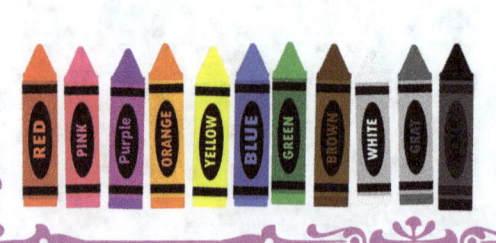

Clothes

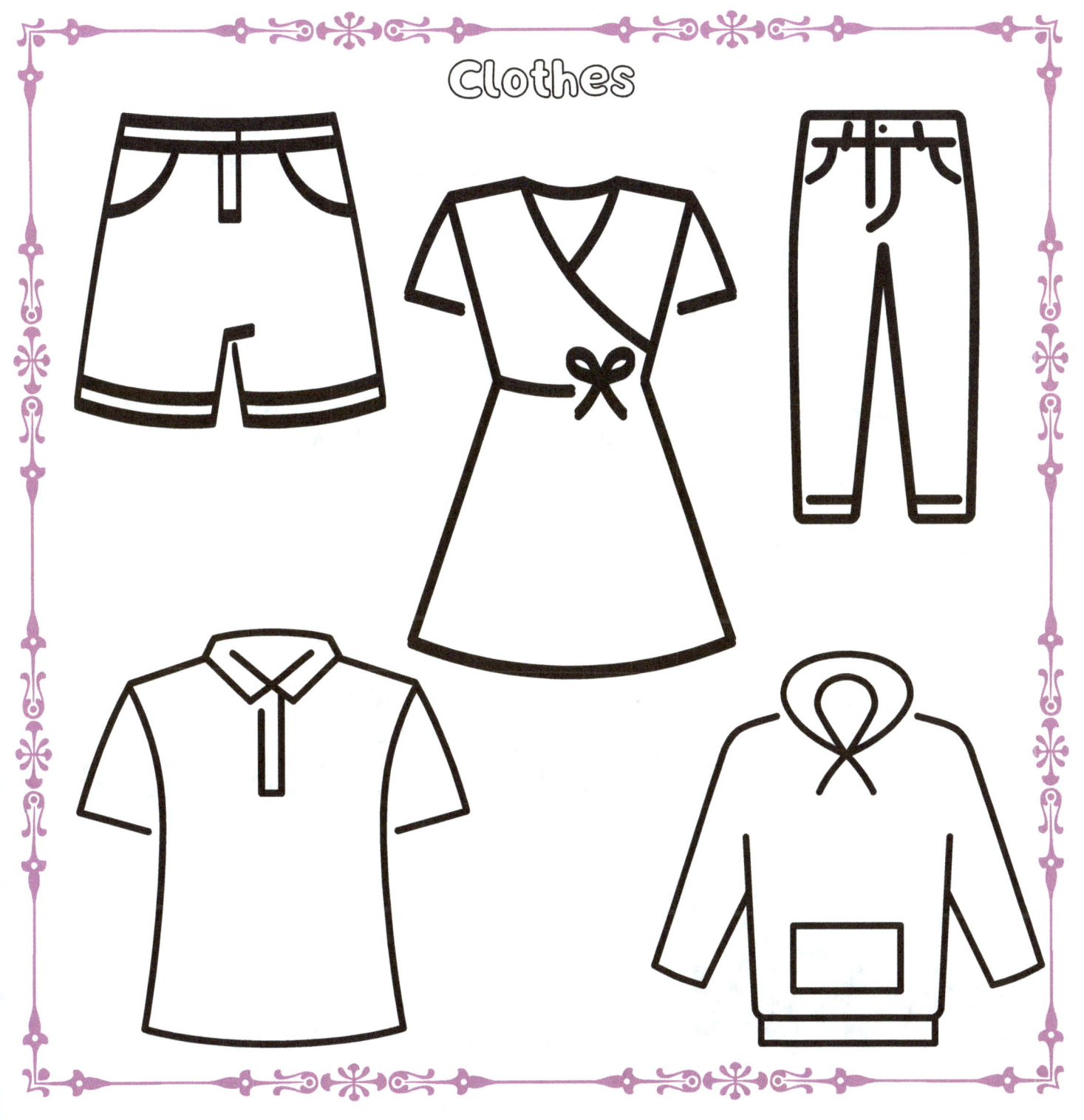

What colors can you find?

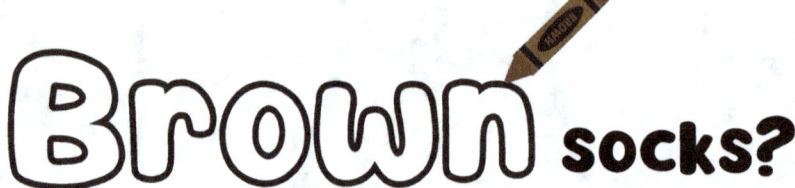 **Brown** socks?

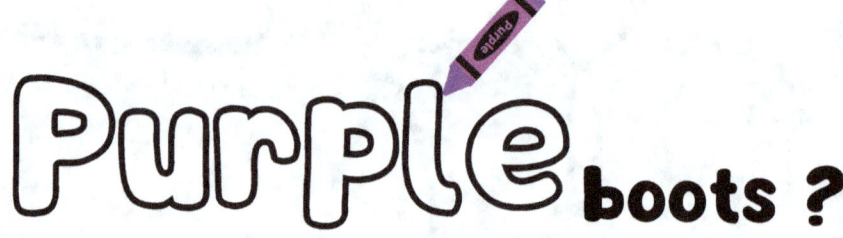 **Purple** boots ?

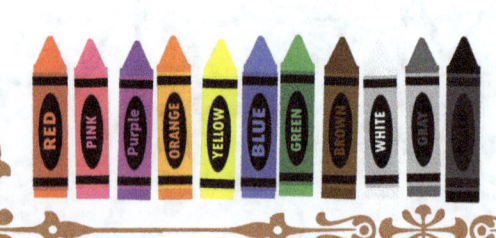

Clothes and shoes

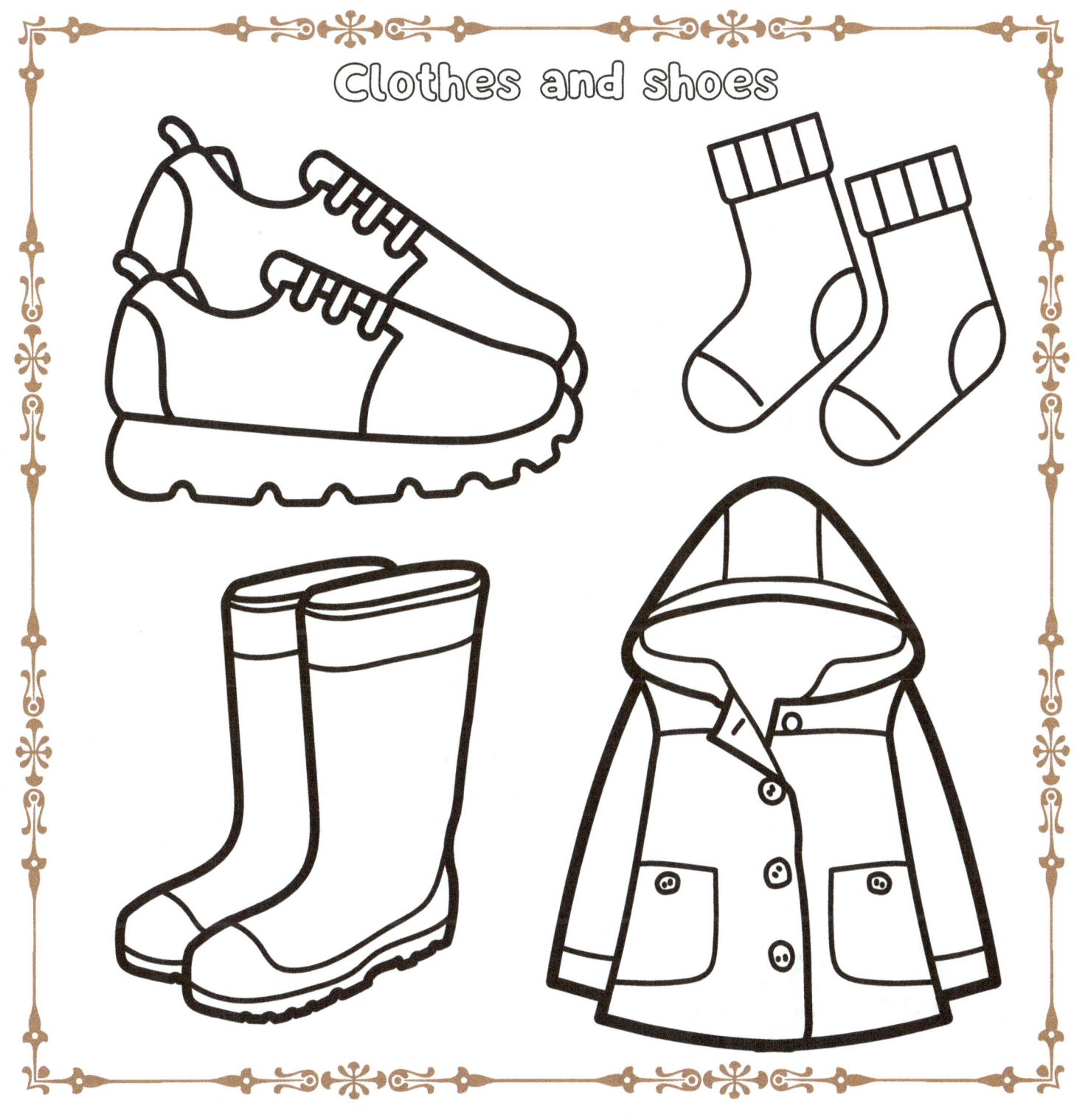

What colors can you find?

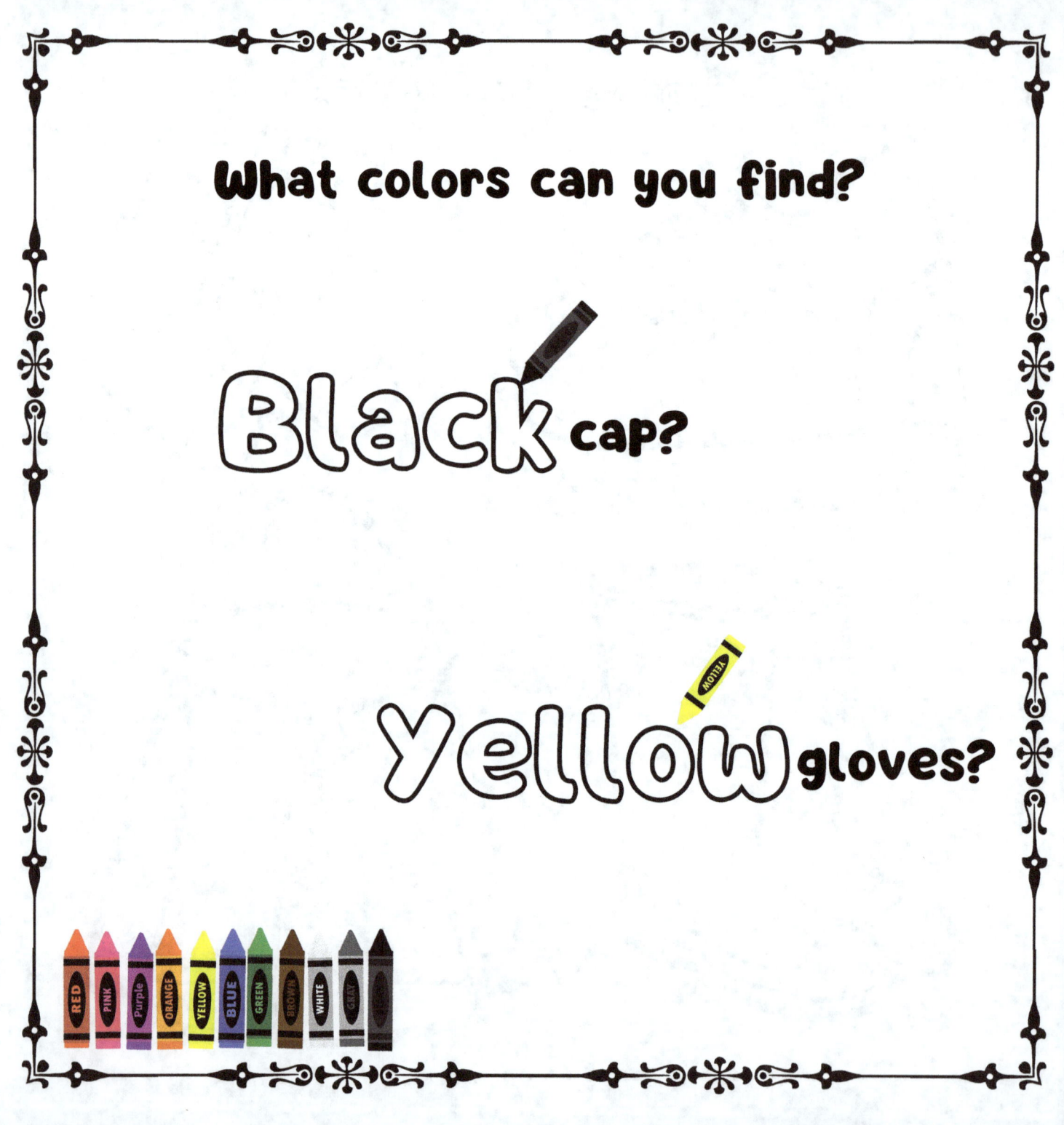

Black cap?

Yellow gloves?

Clothing accessories

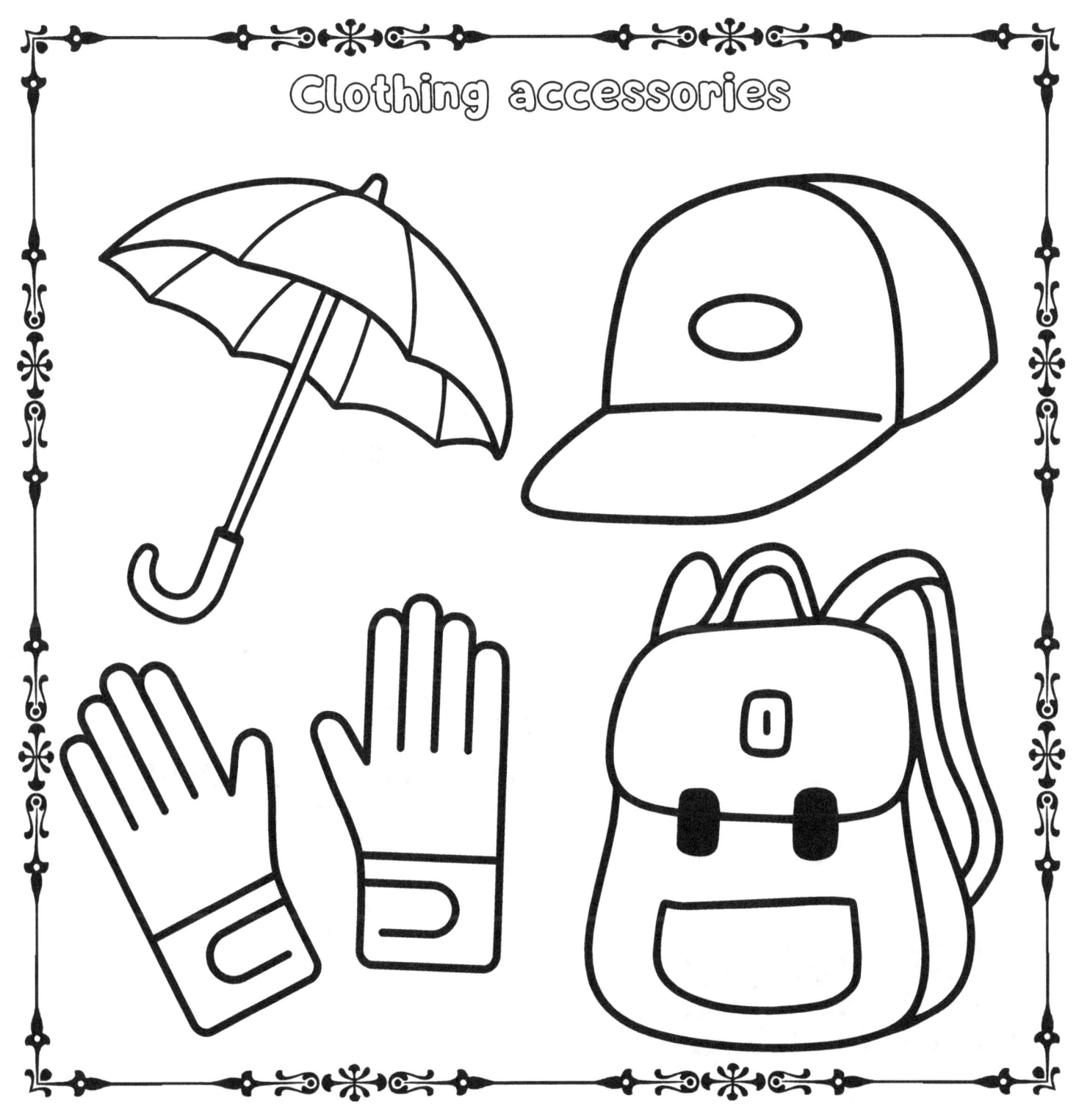

What colors can you find?

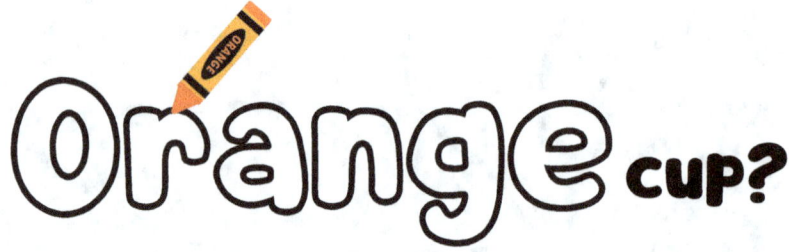 Orange cup?

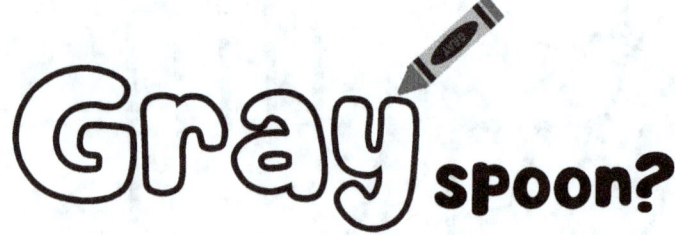 Gray spoon?

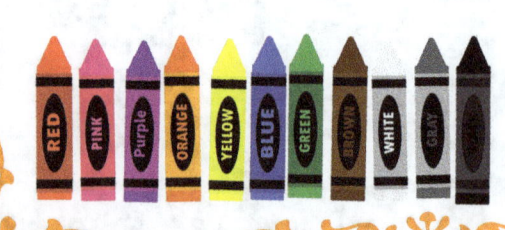

Tableware

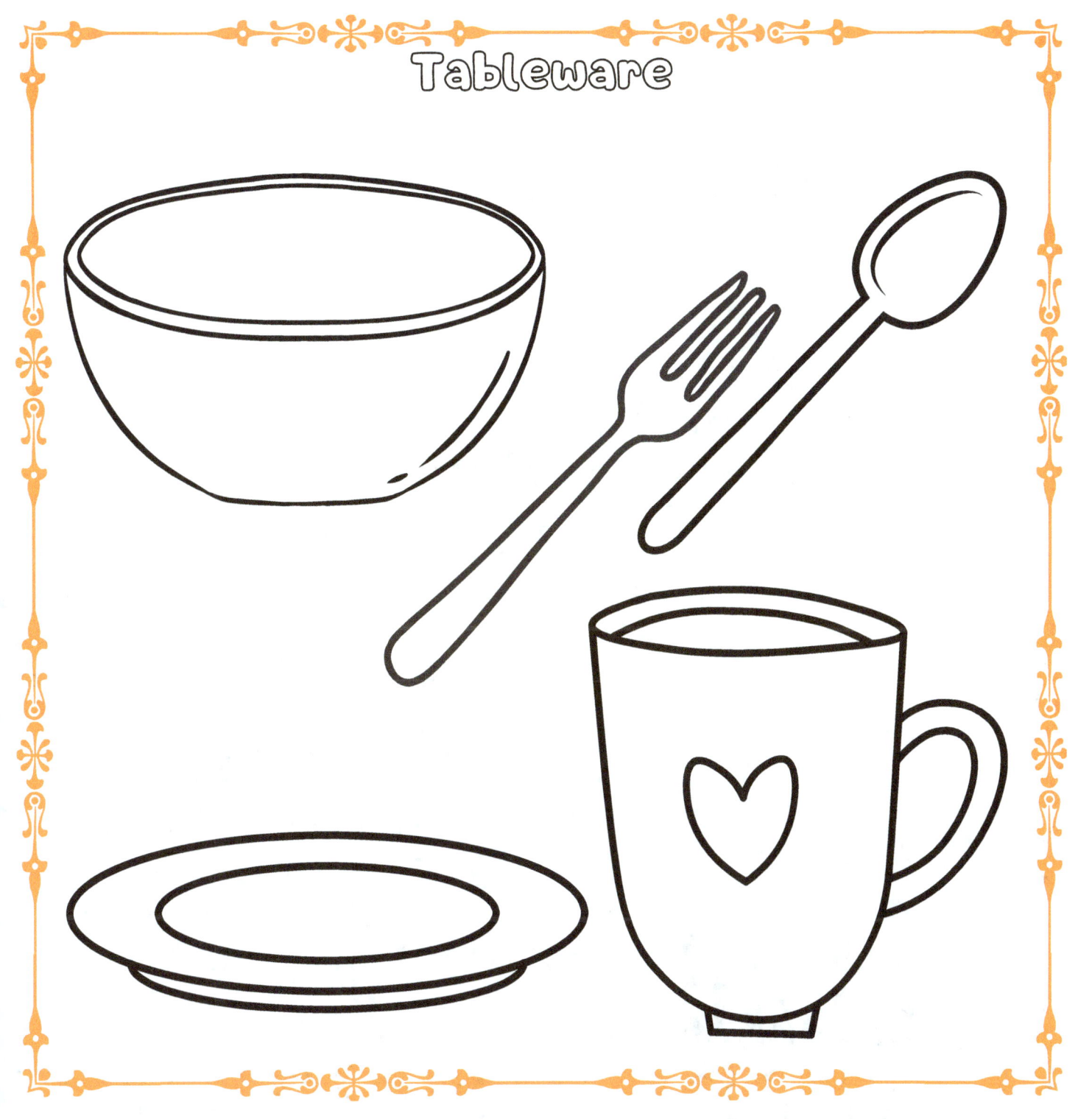

What colors can you find?

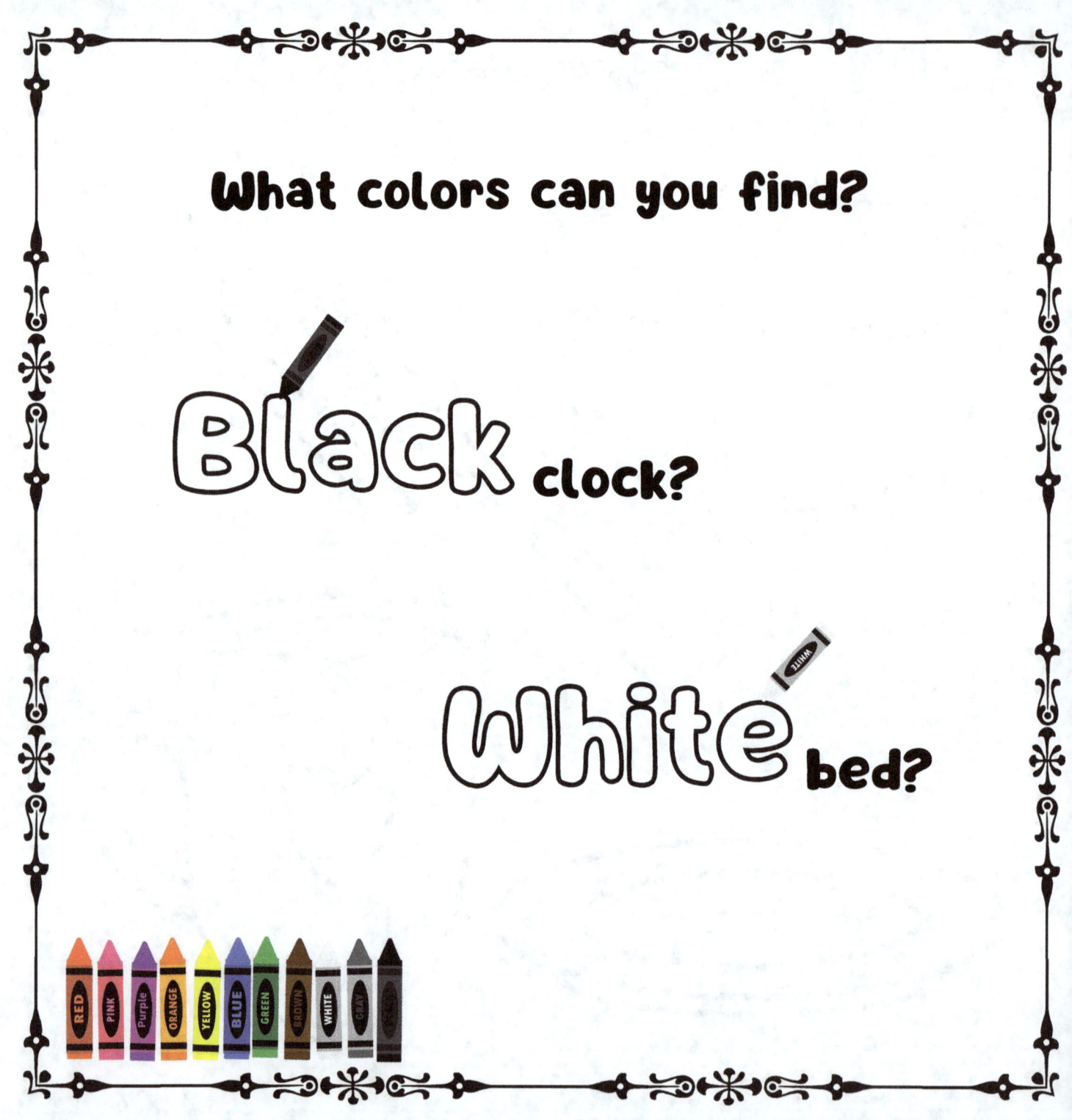

Black clock?

White bed?

Furniture

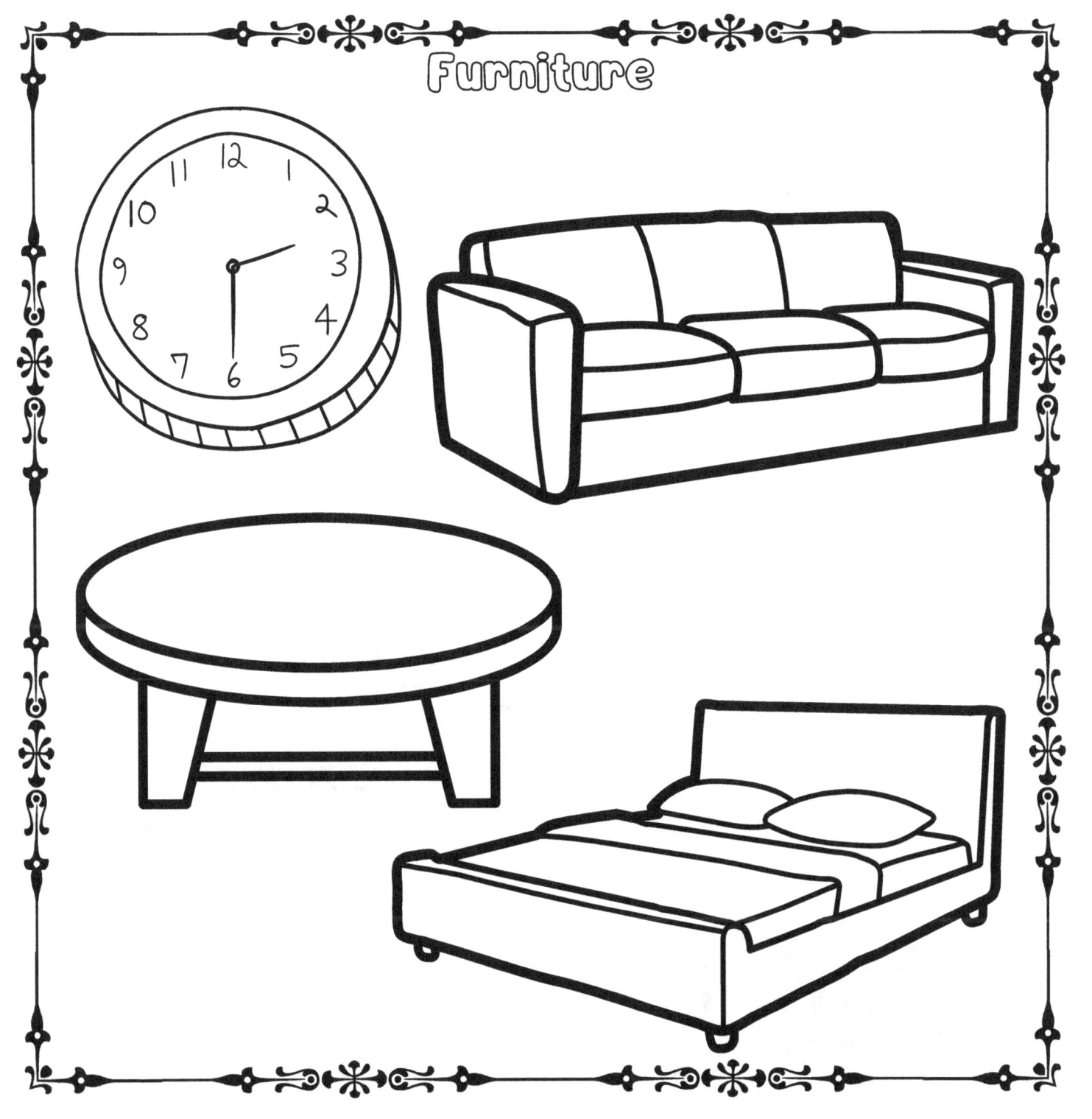

What colors can you find?

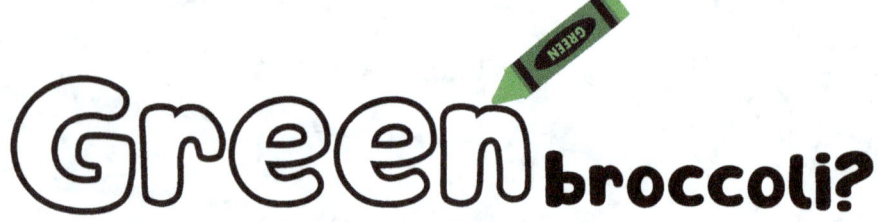 Green broccoli?

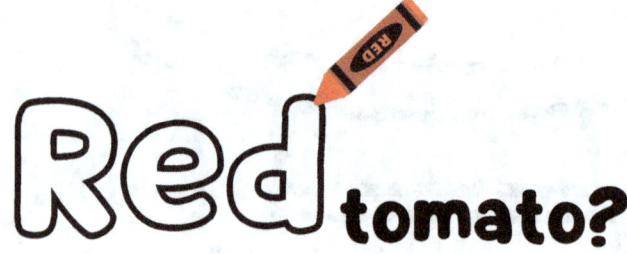 Red tomato?

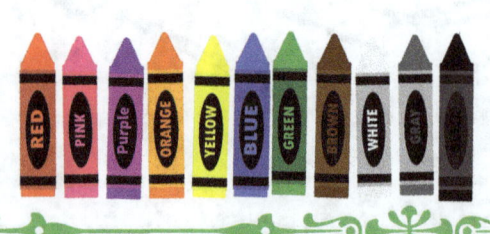

Vegetables

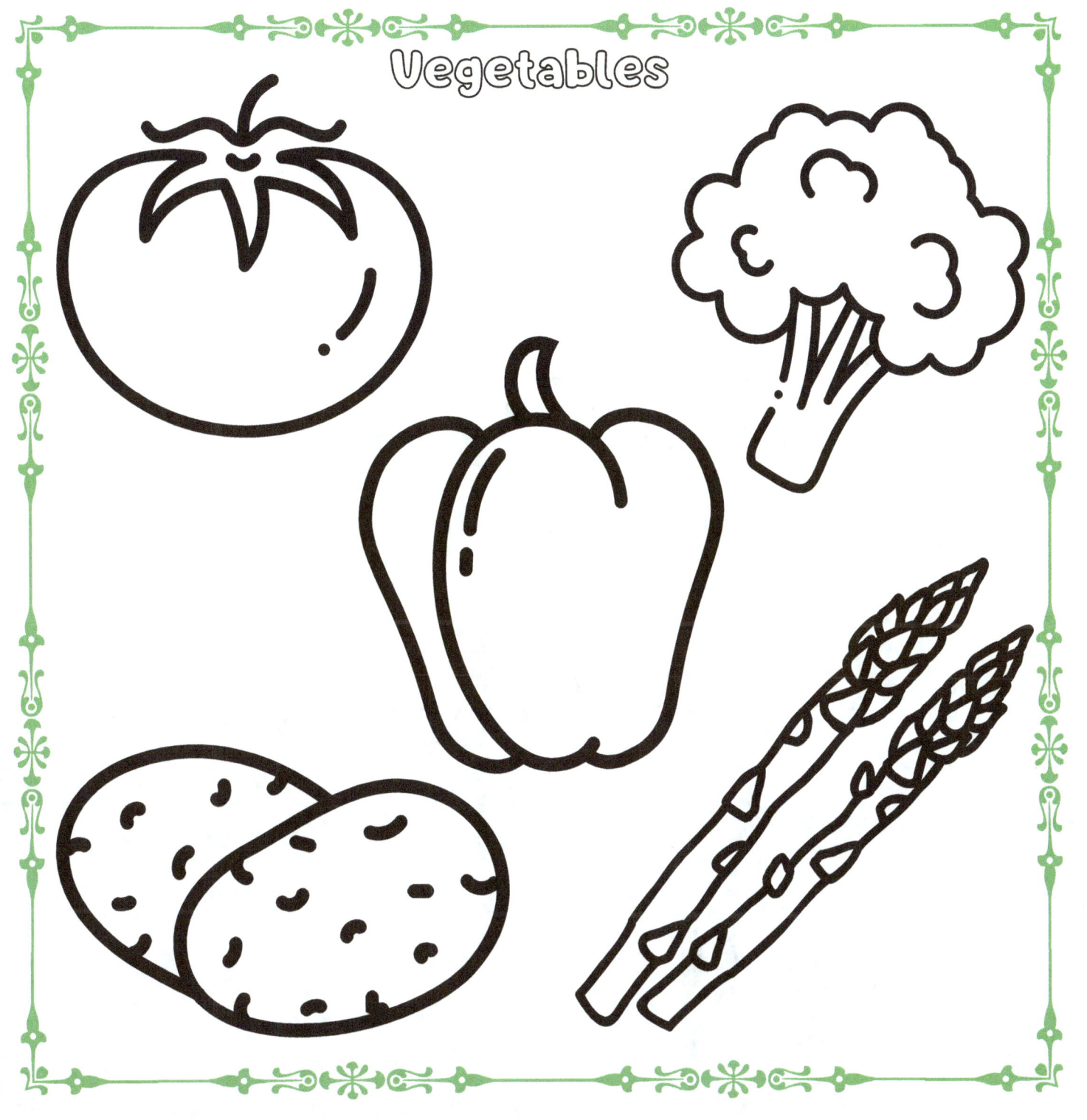

What colors can you find?

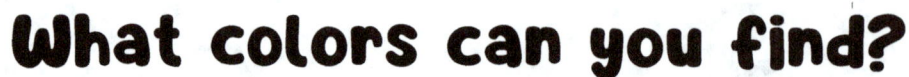

Yellow corn?

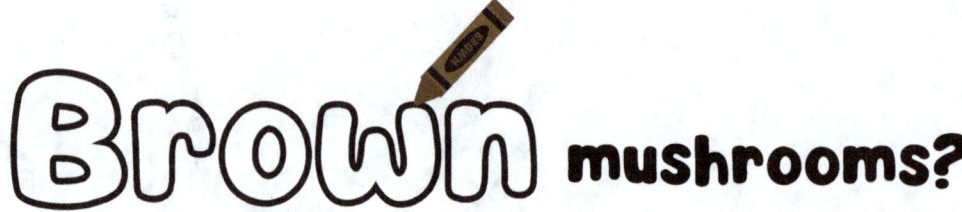

Brown mushrooms?

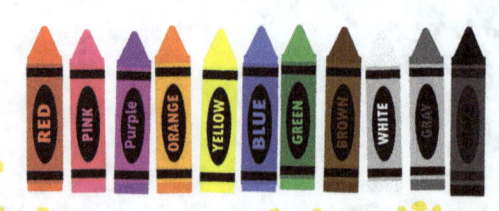

Vegetables

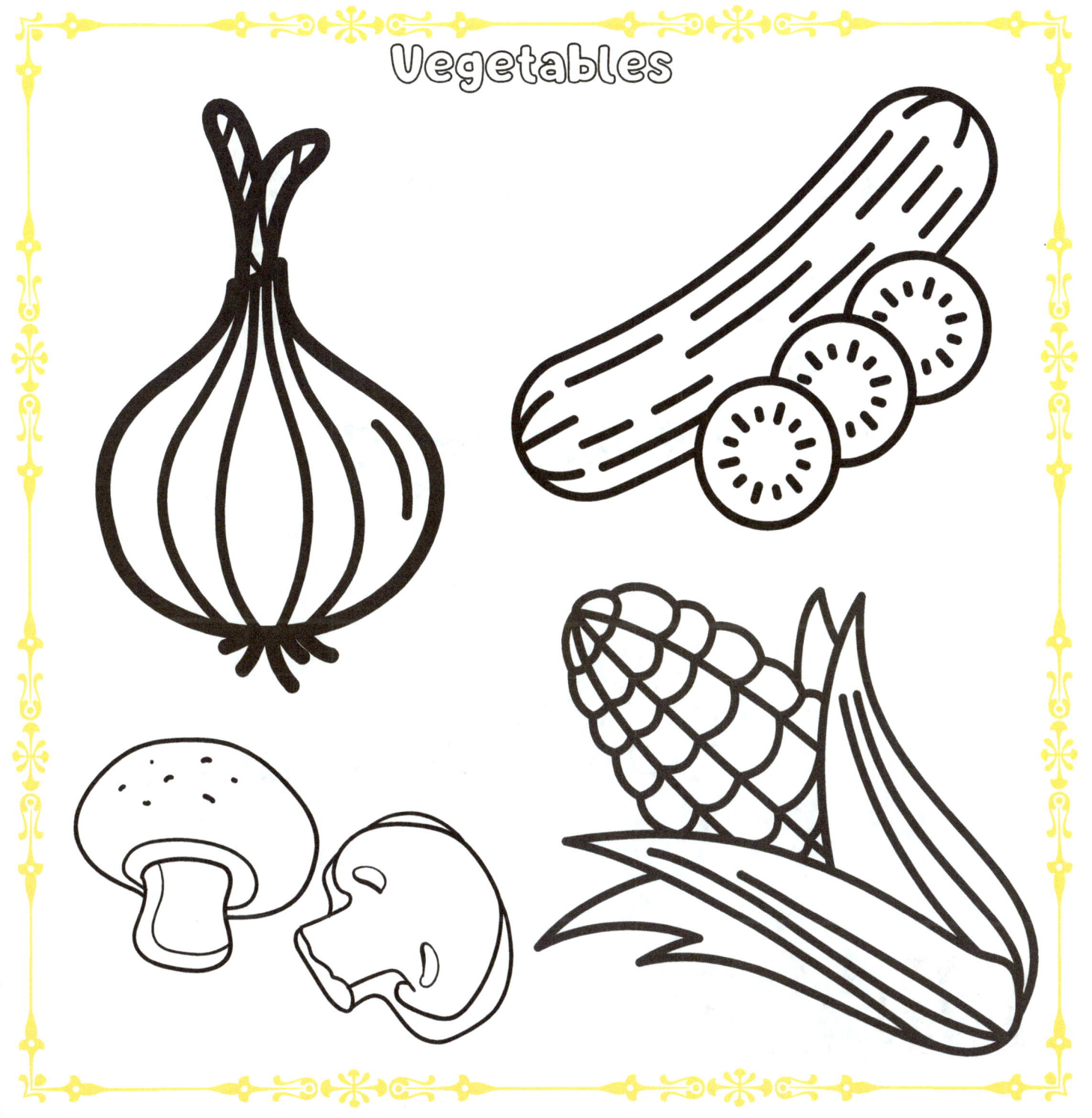

What colors can you find?

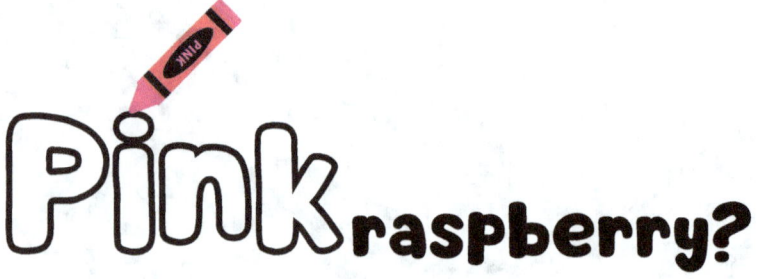

Pink raspberry?

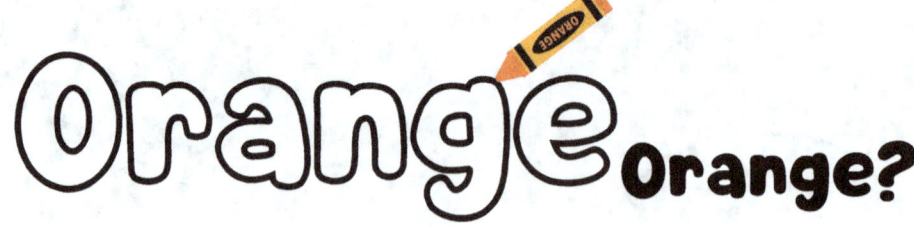

Orange Orange?

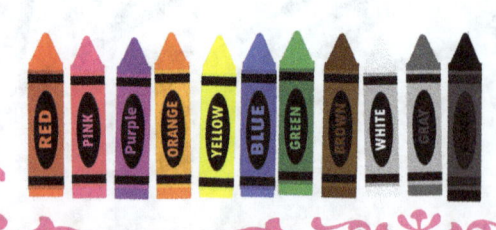

Fruits

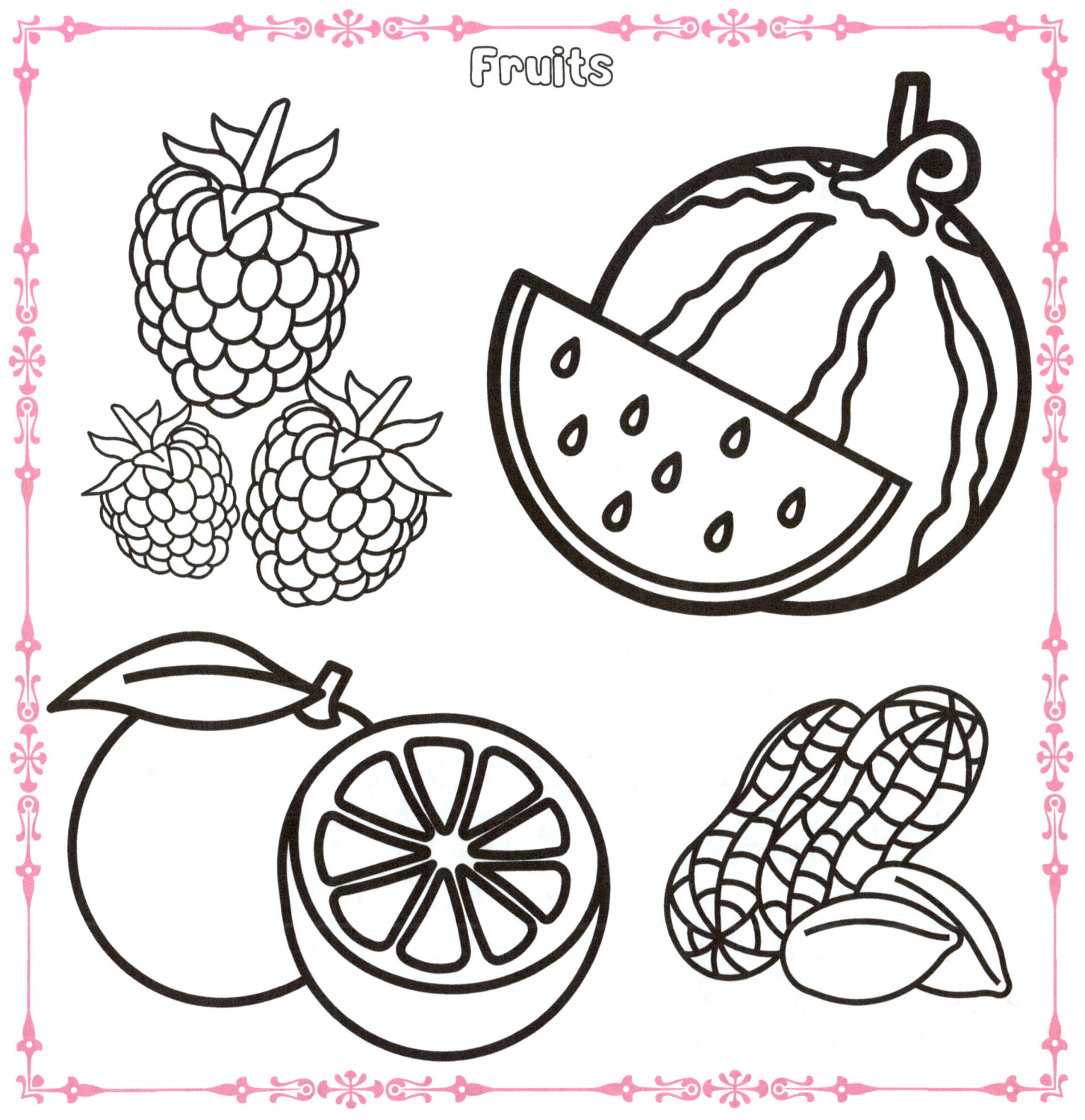

What colors can you find?

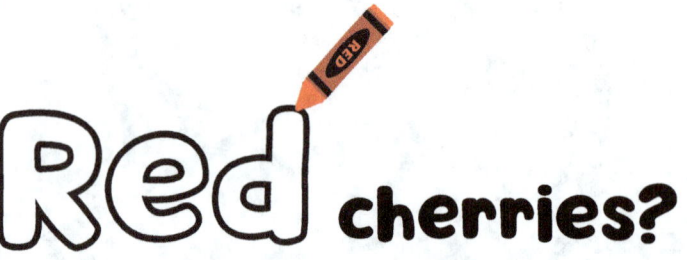 **cherries?**

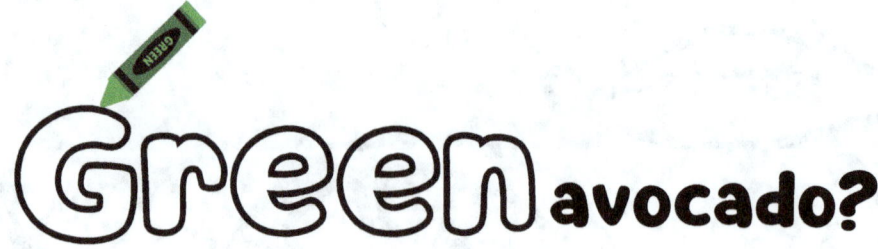 **avocado?**

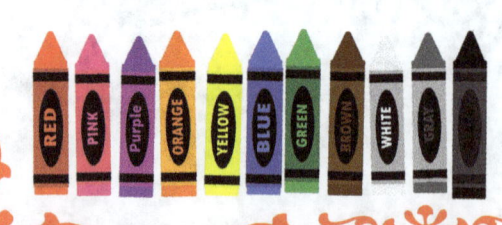

Fruits

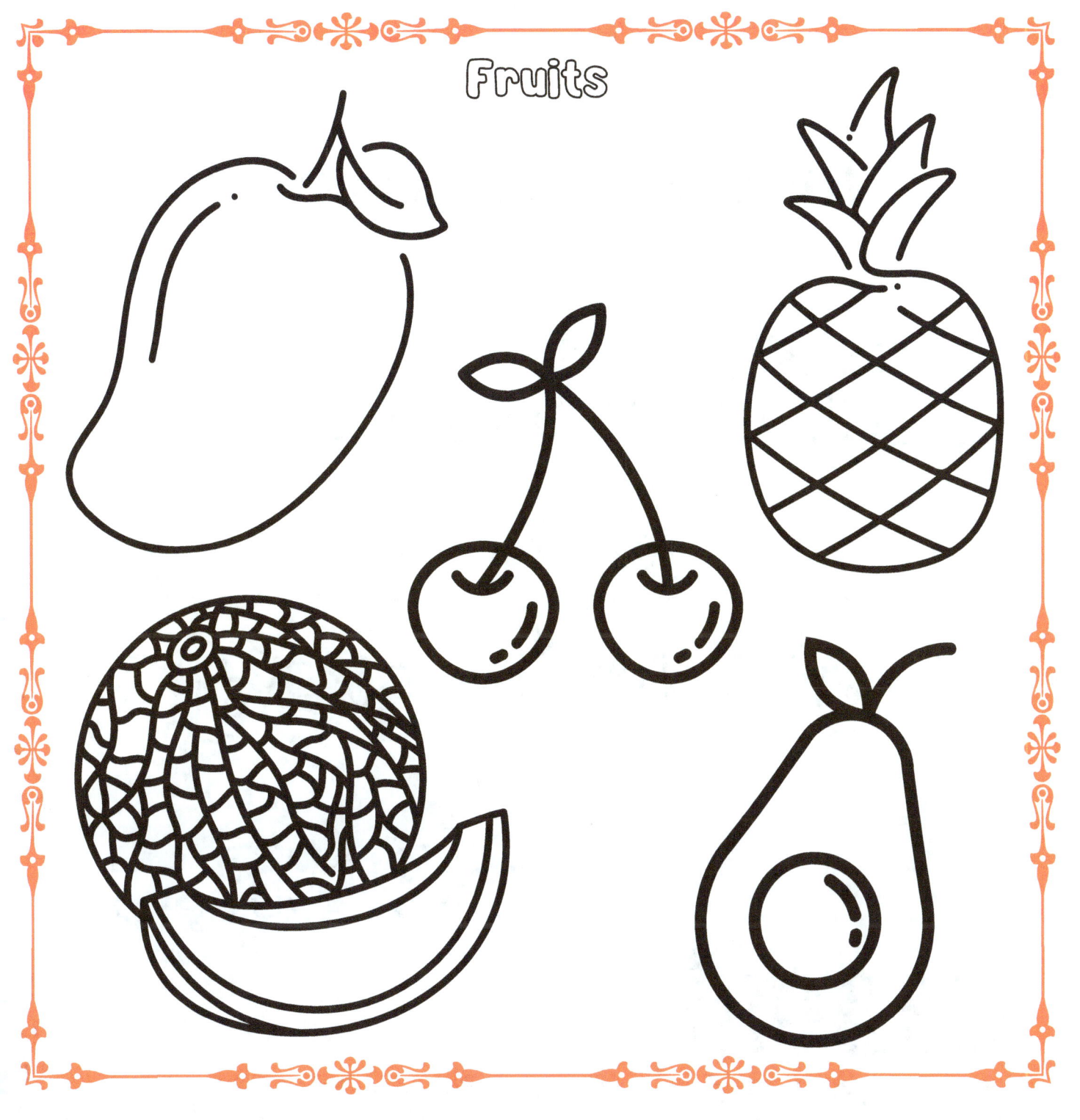

What colors can you find?

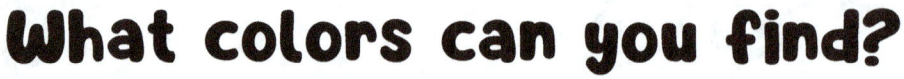

Brown pancake?

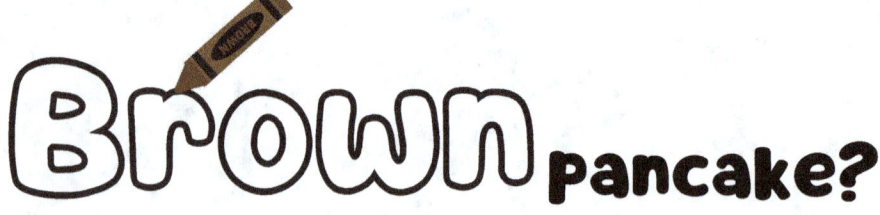

Yellow, red, brown pizza?

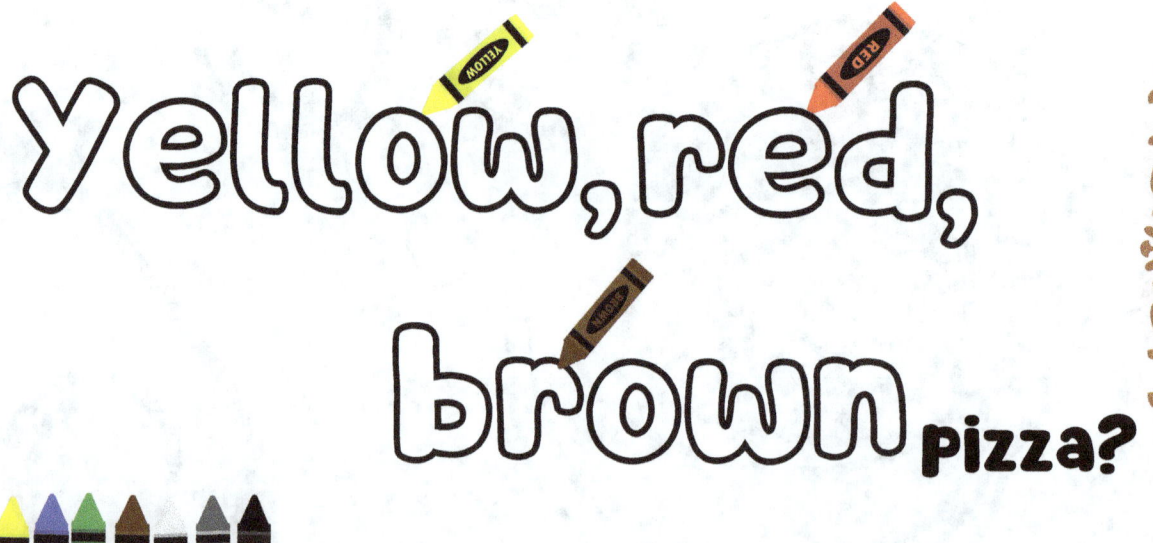

Foods

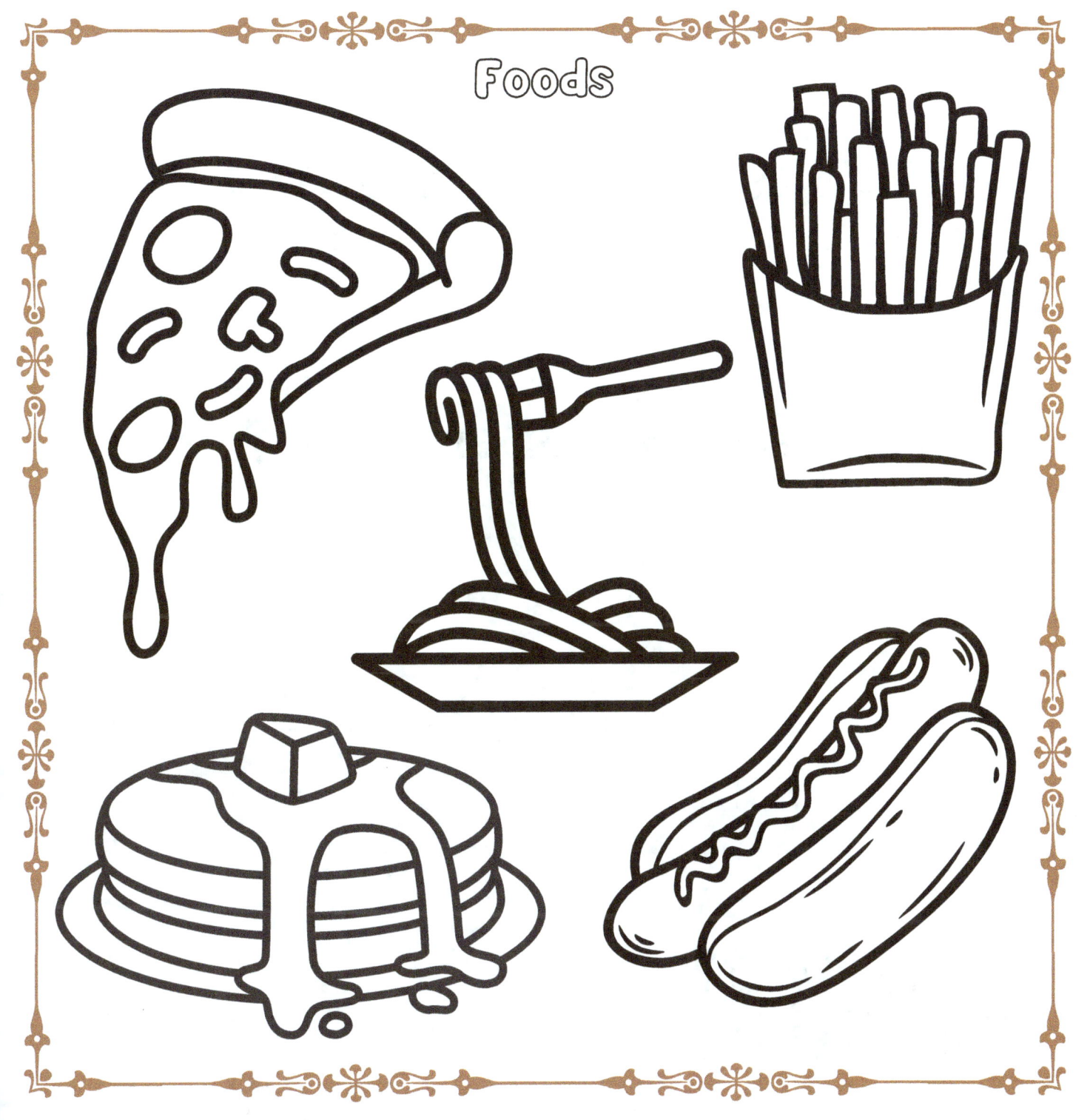

What colors can you find?

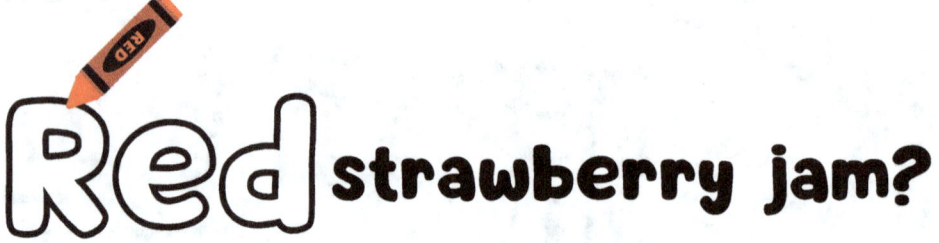 **Red** strawberry jam?

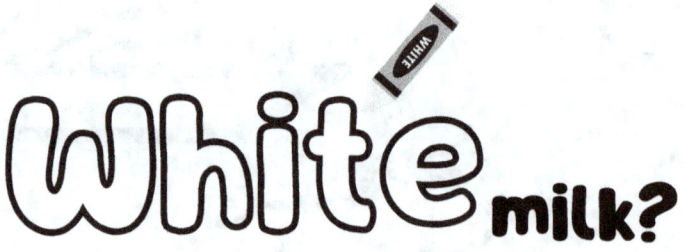 **White** milk?

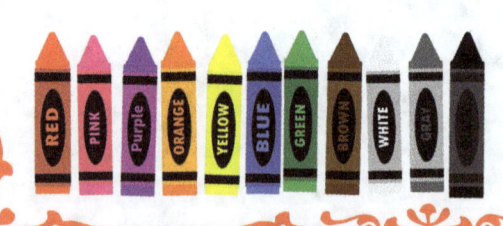

Foods

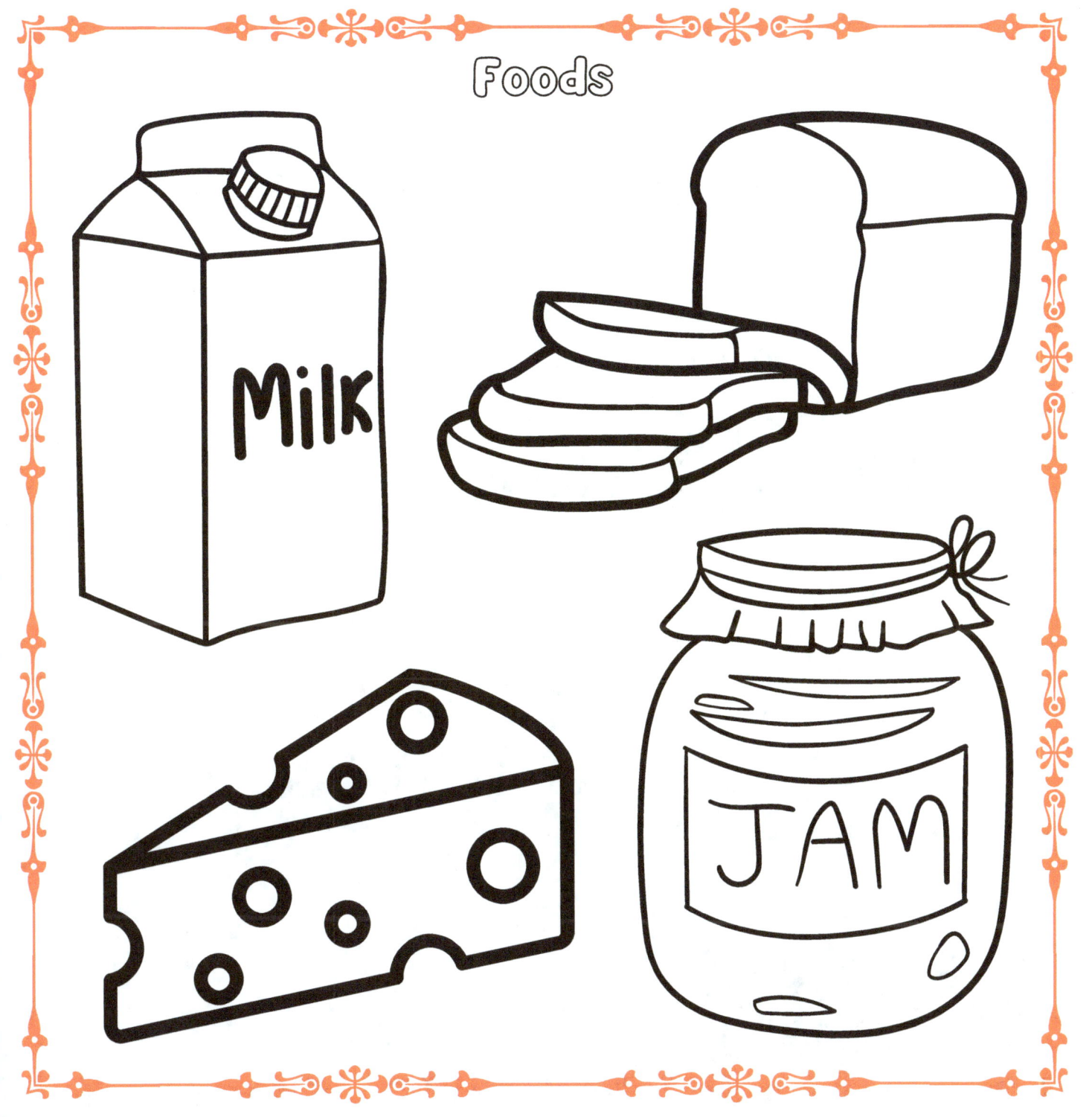

What colors can you find?

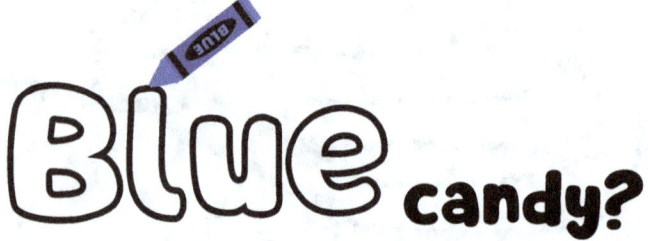 **Blue** candy?

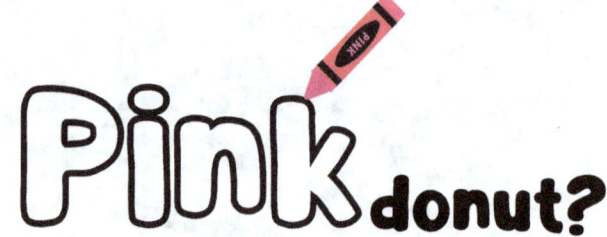 **Pink** donut?

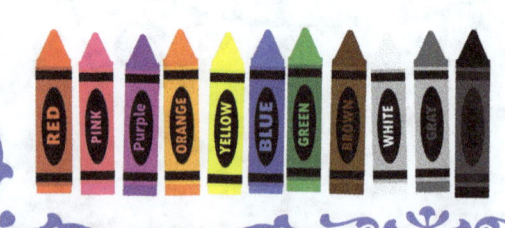

Sweets

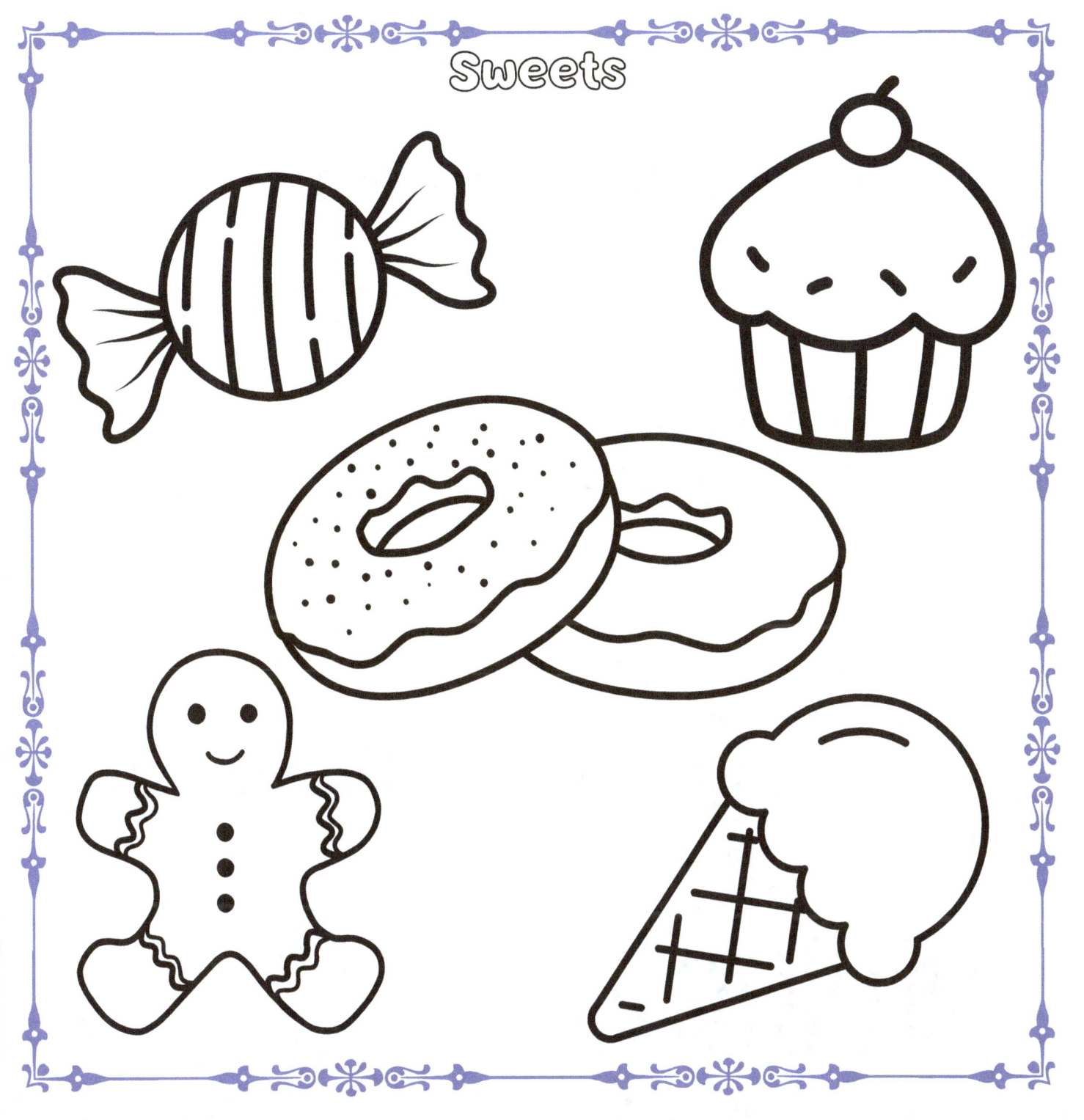

What colors can you find?

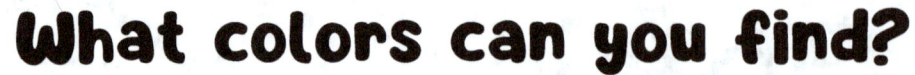

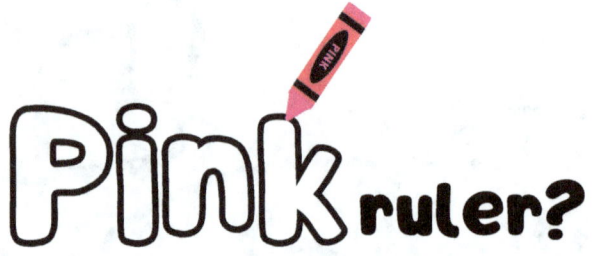 **ruler?**

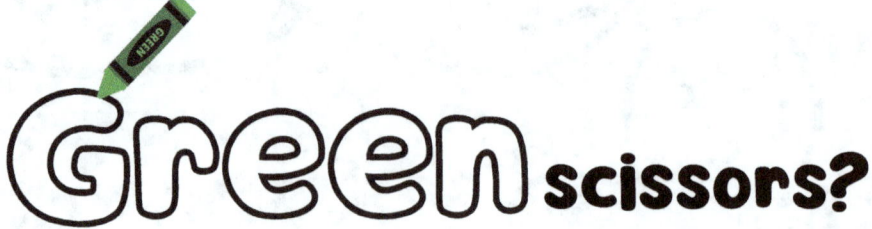 **scissors?**

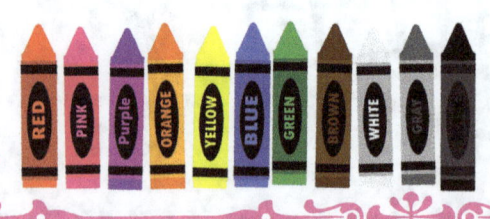

Stationery

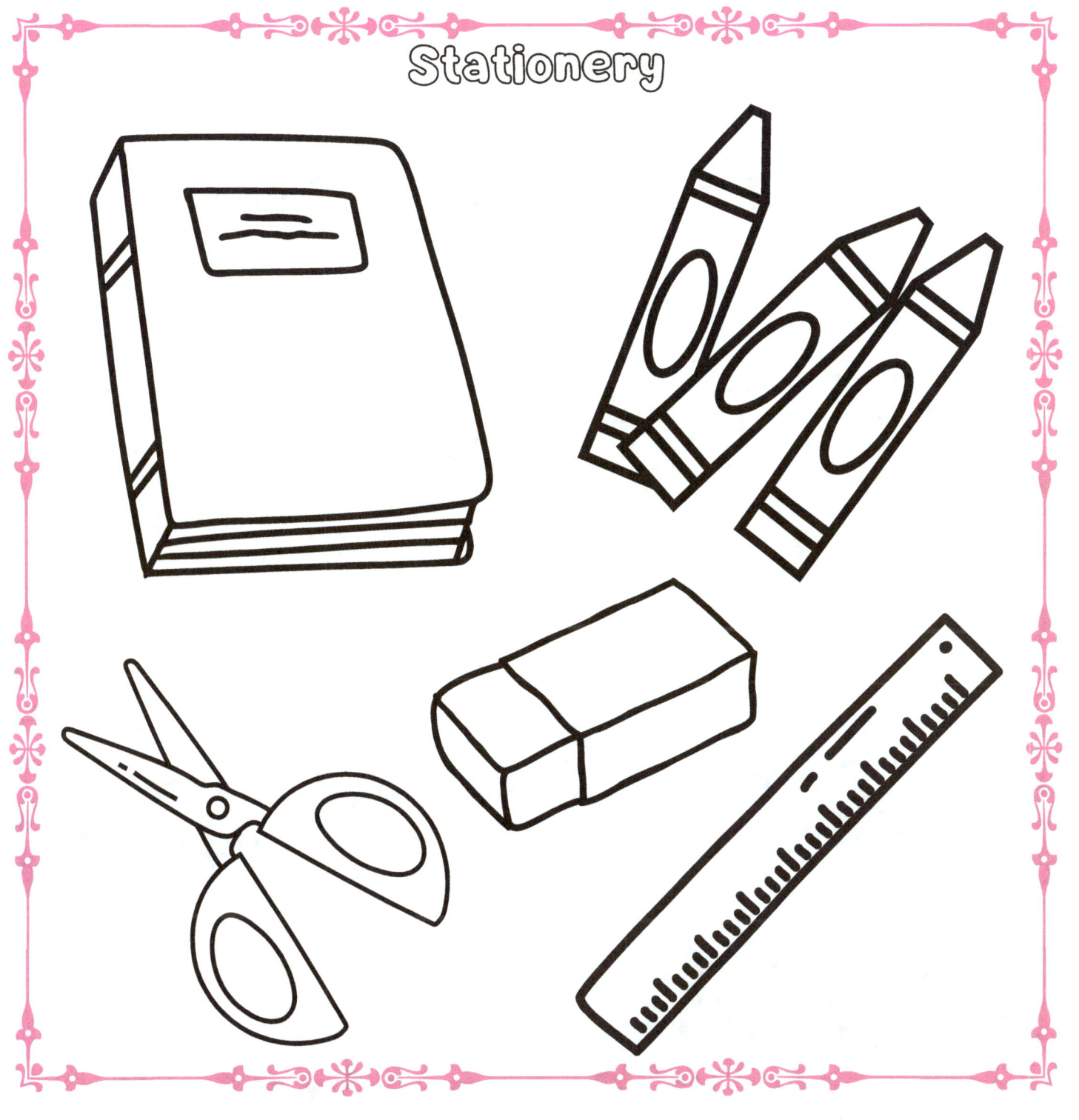

What colors can you find?

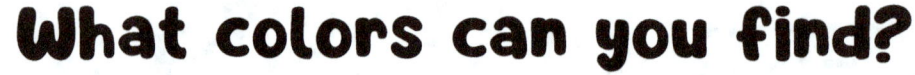

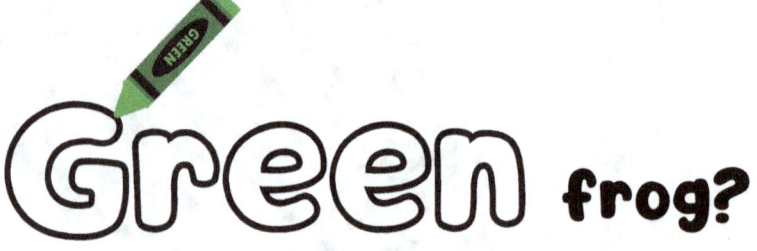 **Green** frog?

Black and **White**

panda?

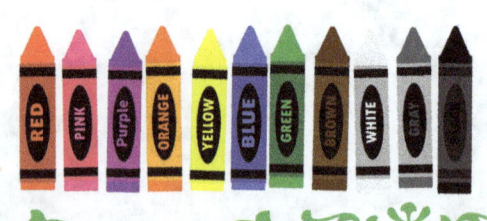

Animals

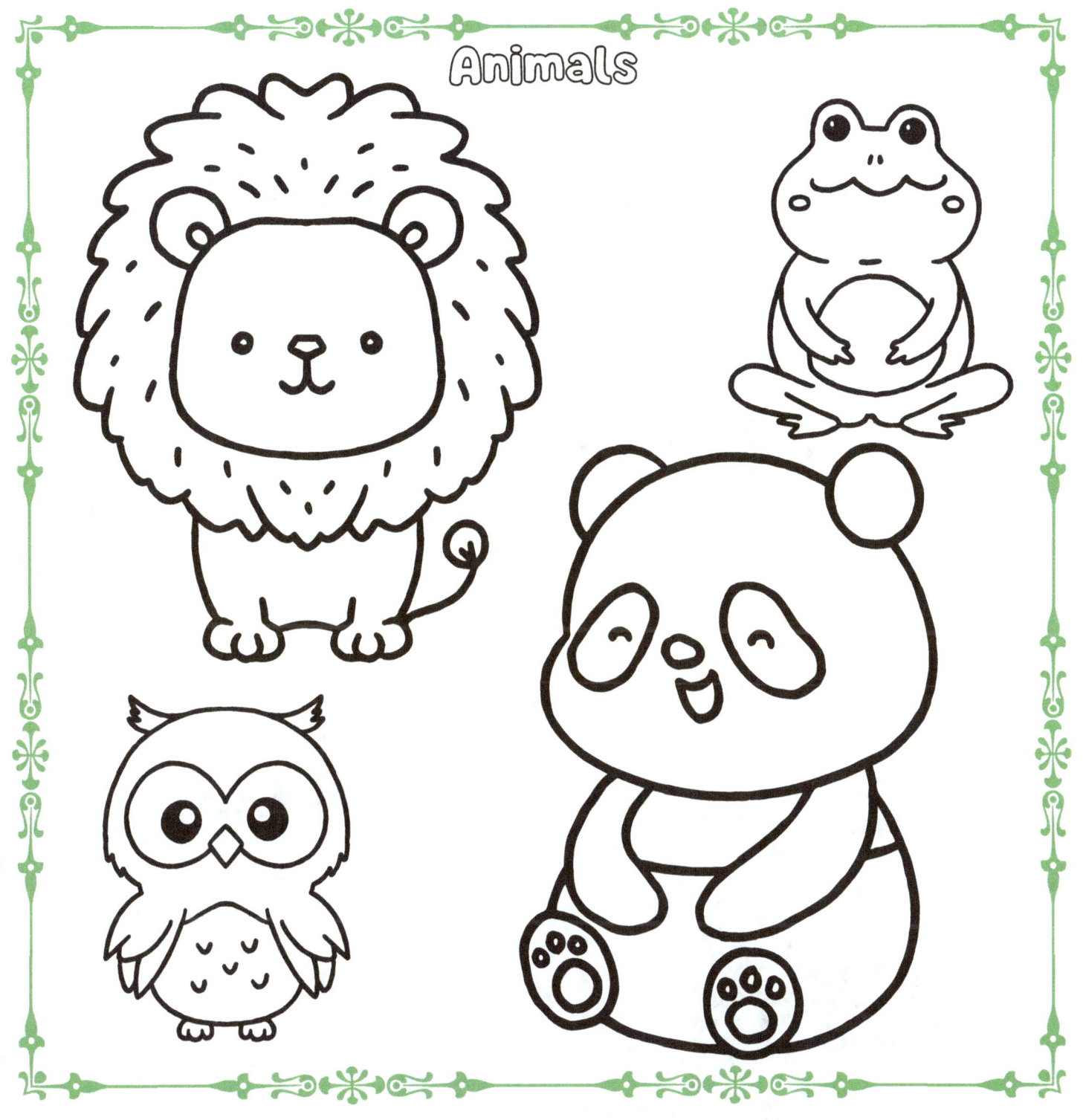

What colors can you find?

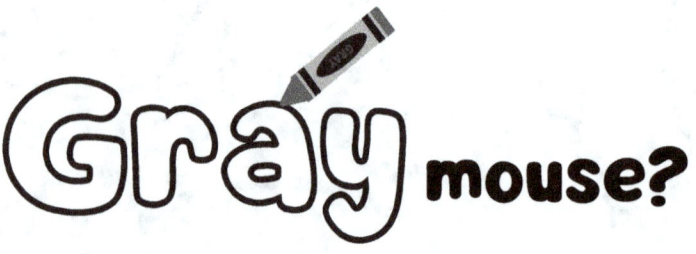 **Gray** mouse?

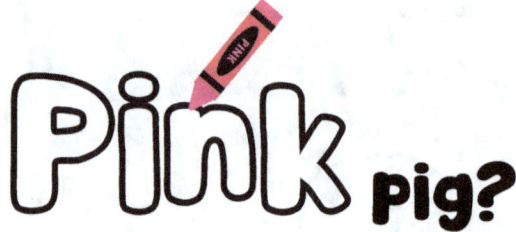 **Pink** pig?

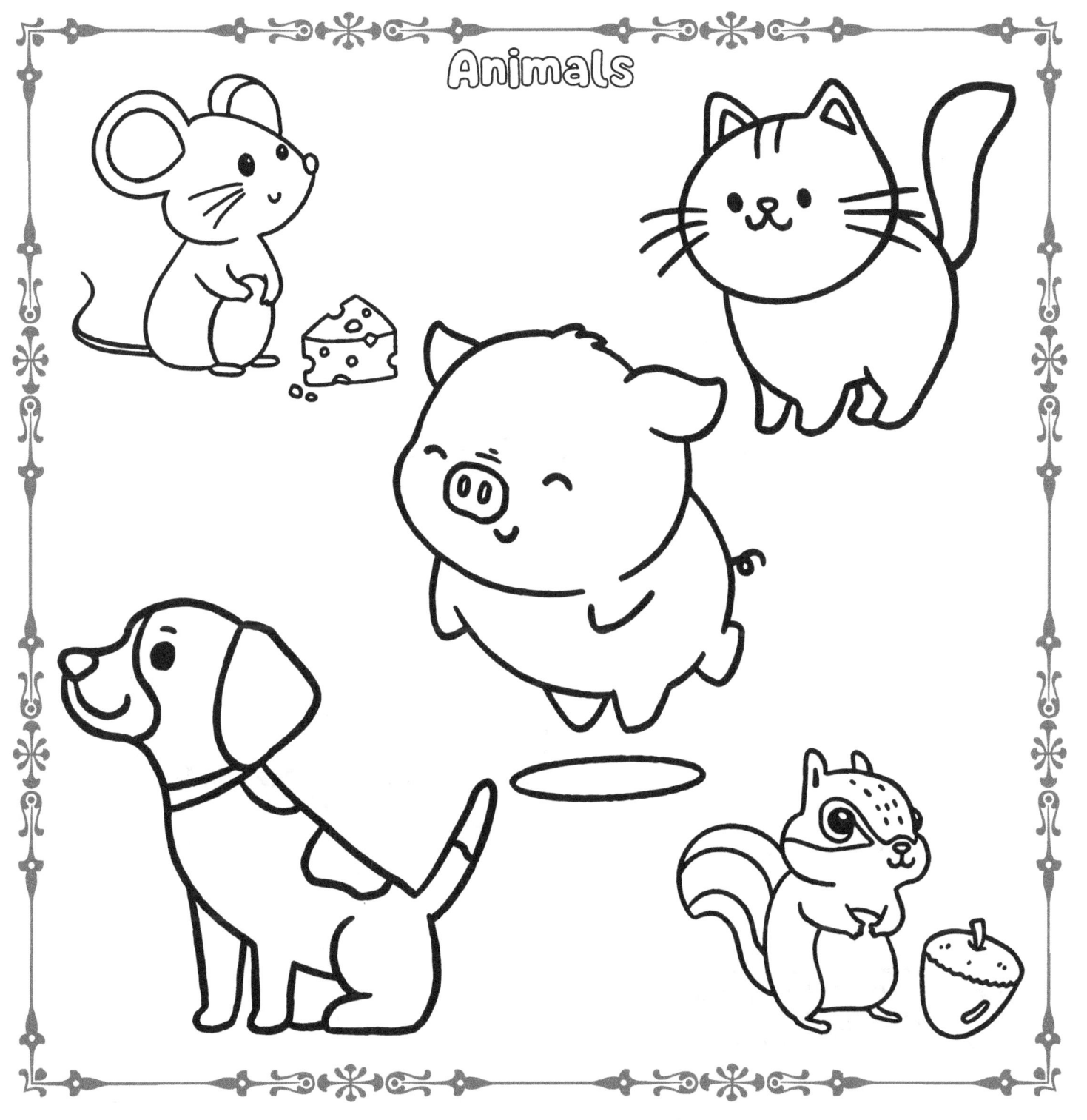

What colors can you find?

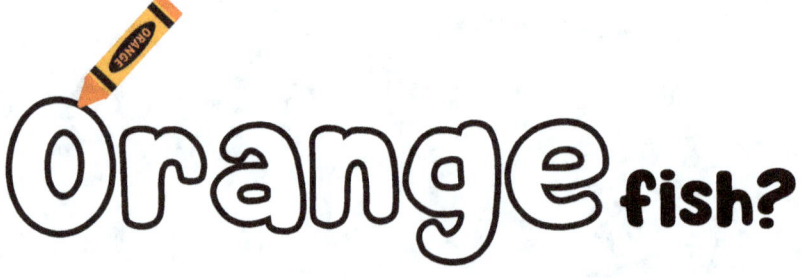

Orange fish?

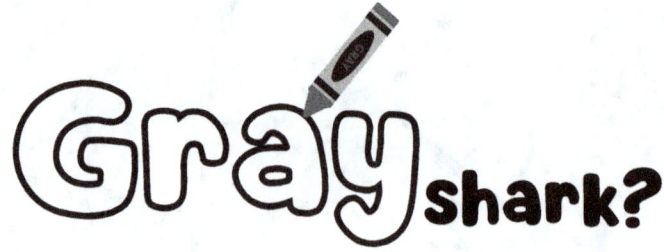

Gray shark?

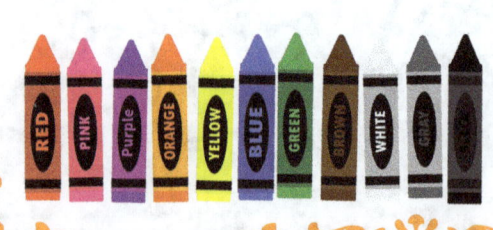

Sea animals

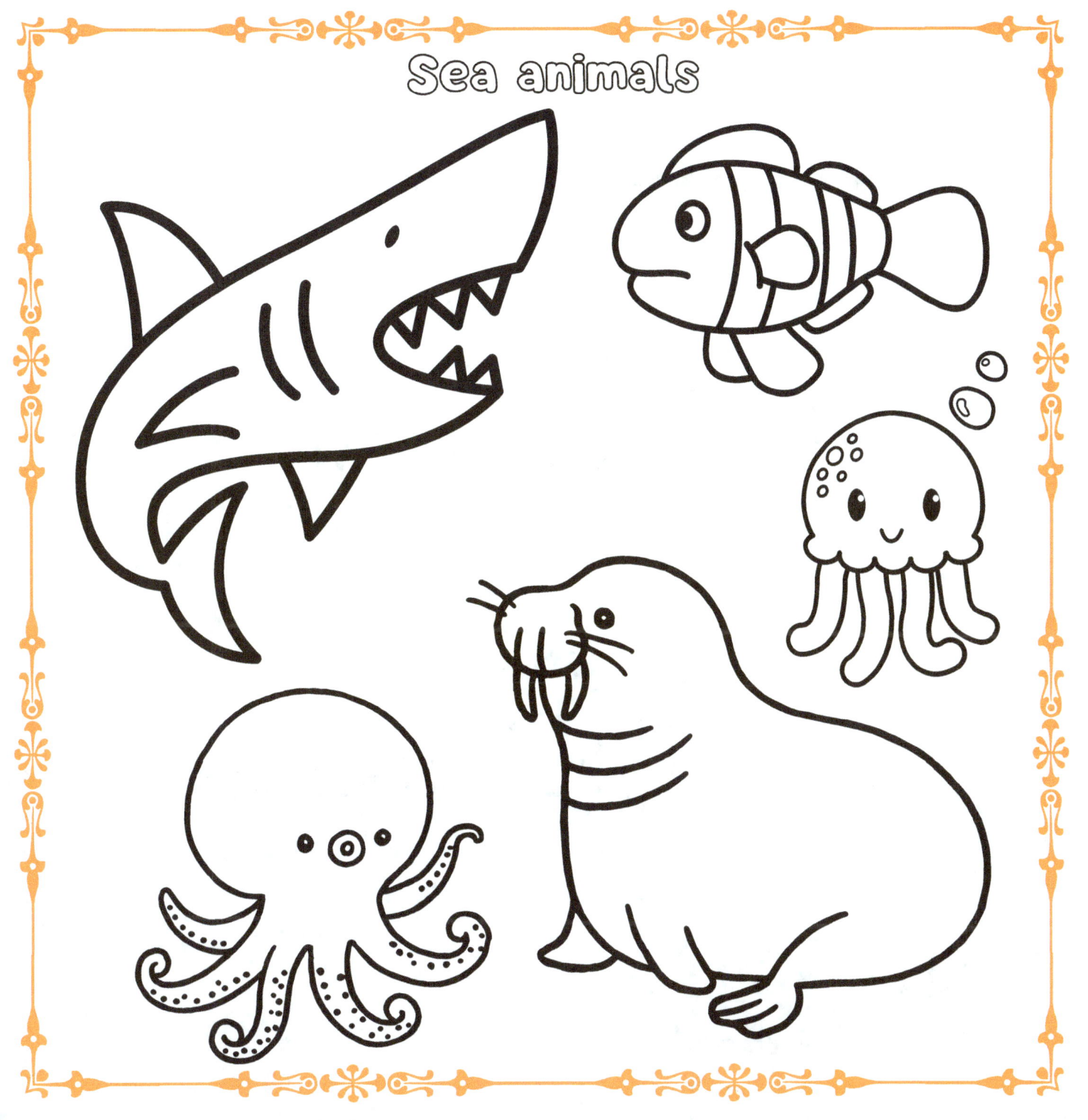

What colors can you find?

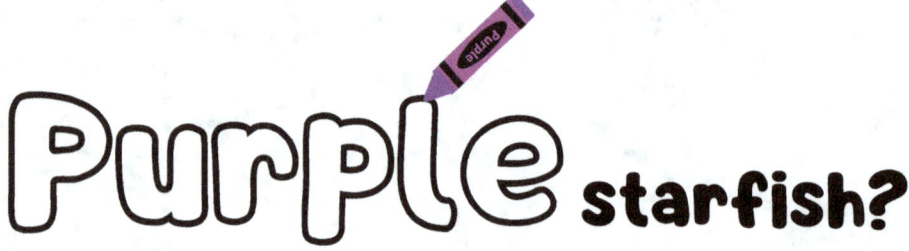 **Purple** starfish?

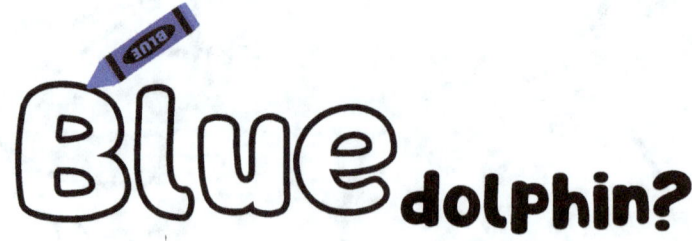 **Blue** dolphin?

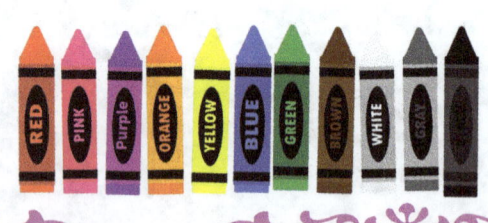

Sea animals

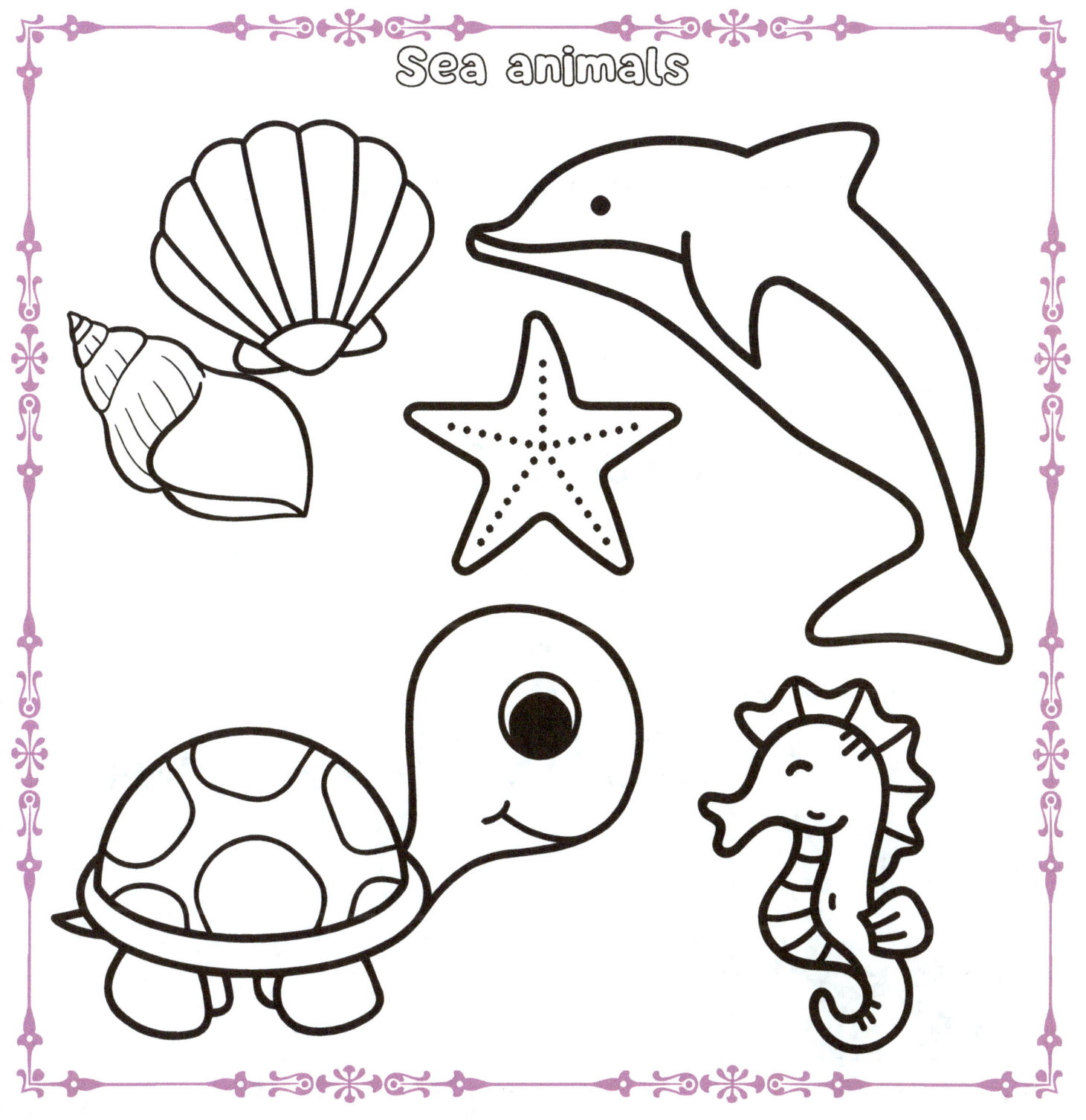

What colors can you find?

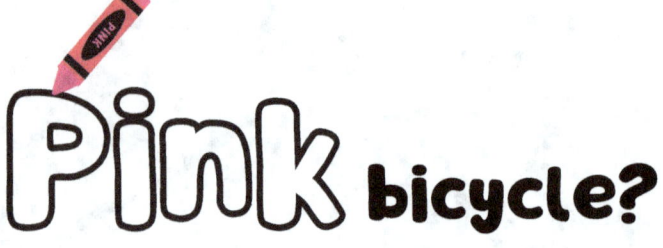 **Pink** bicycle?

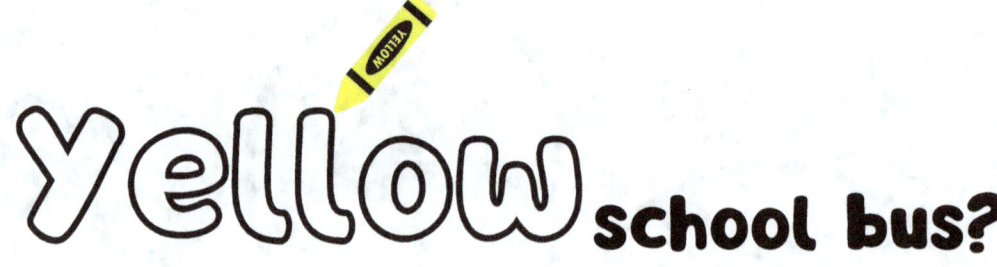 **Yellow** school bus?

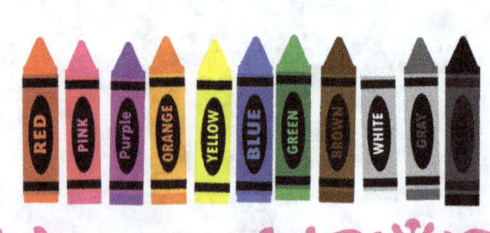

Vehicles

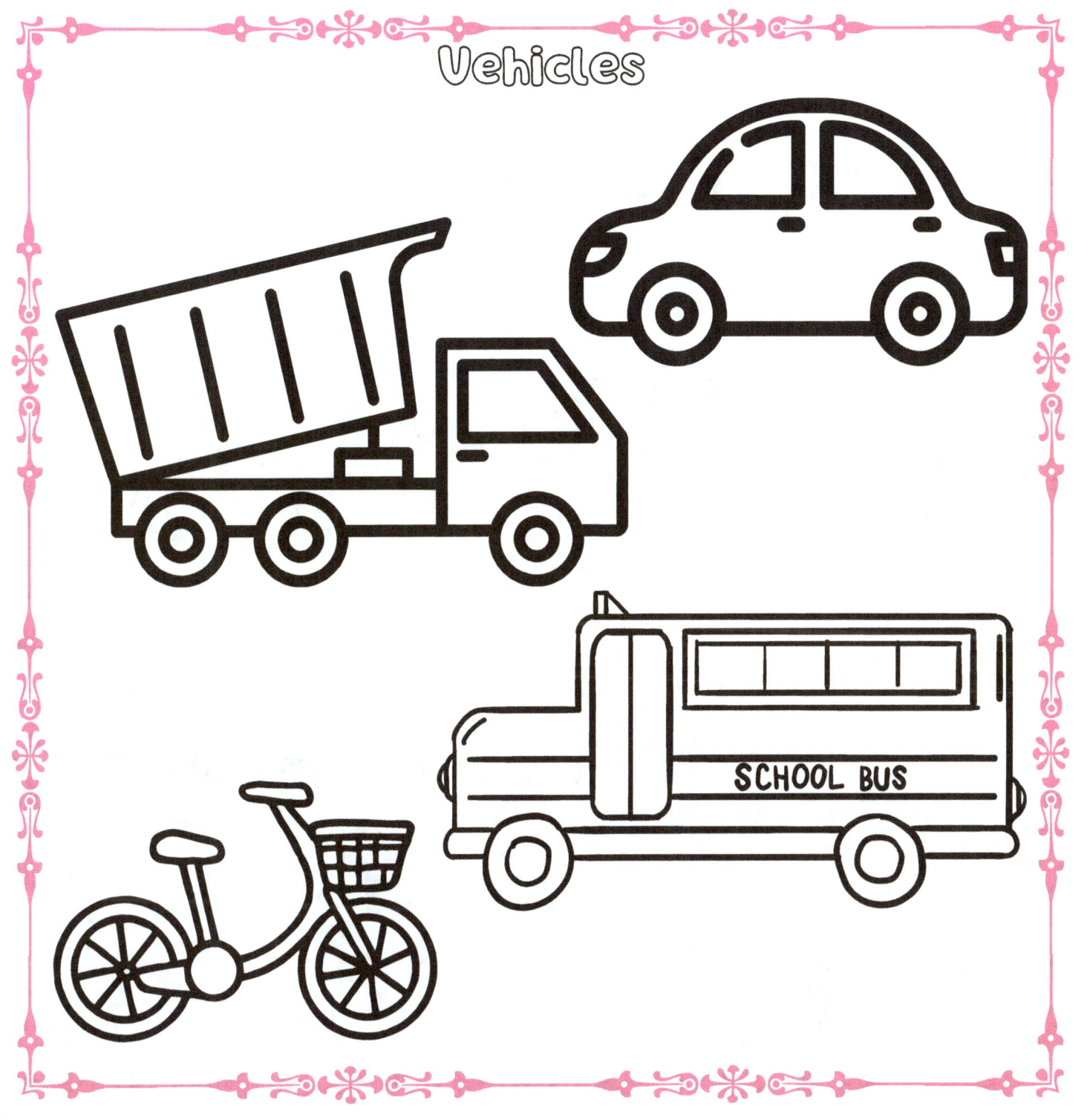

What colors can you find?

Brown ship?

White airplane?

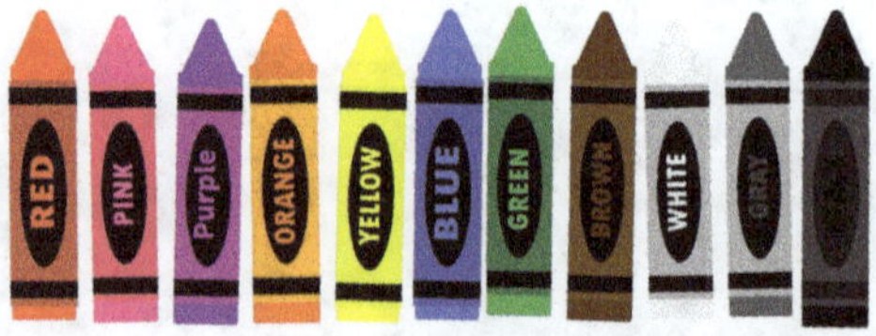

Vehicles

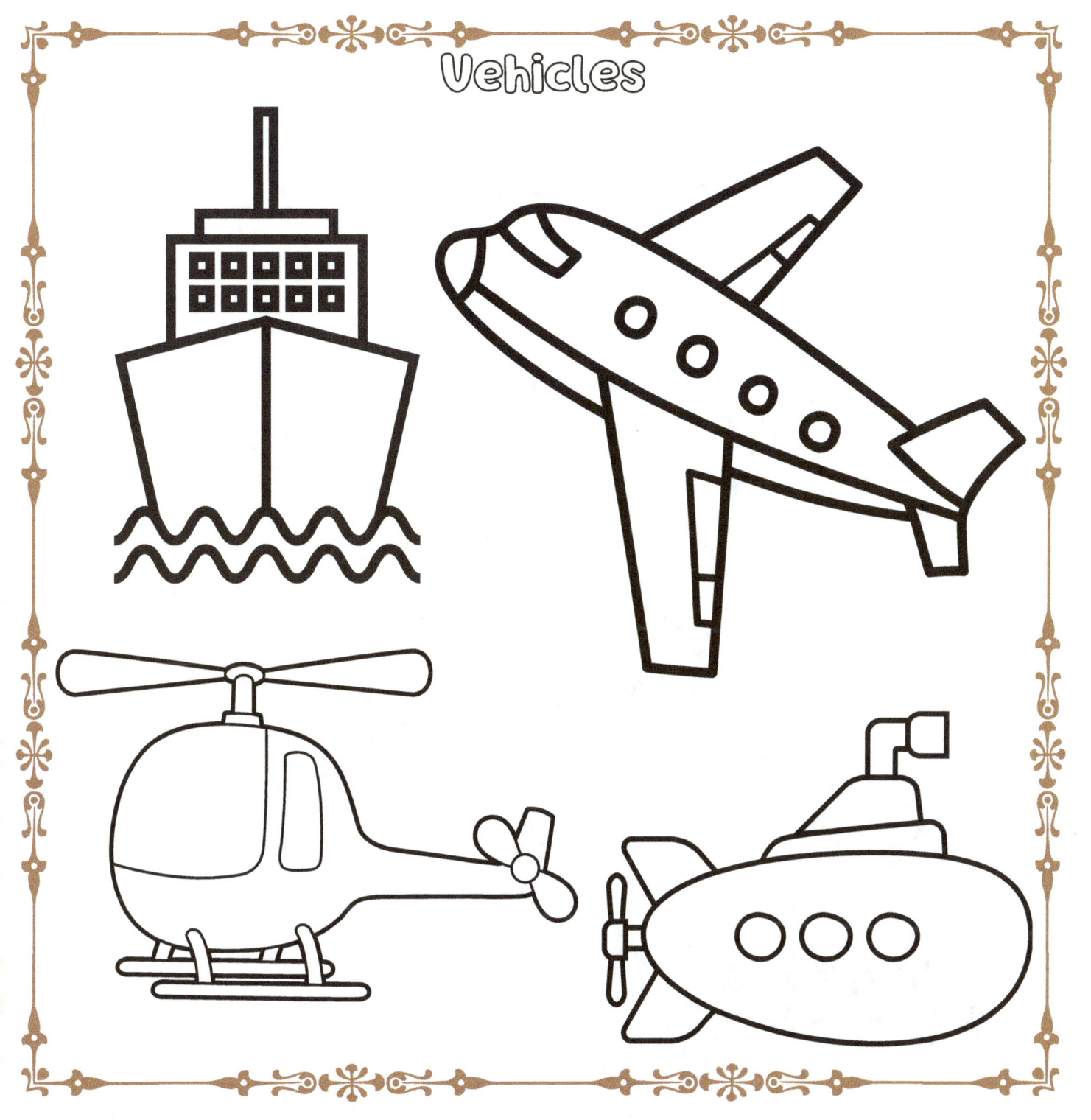

What colors can you find?

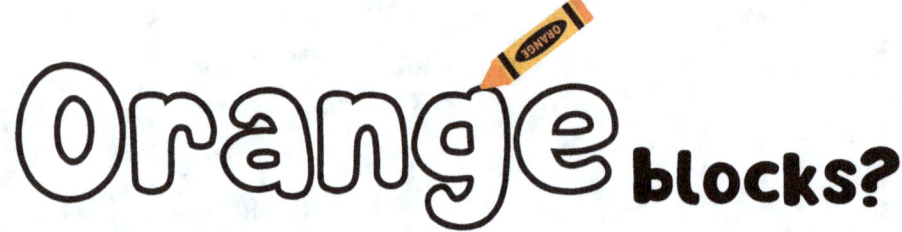

Orange blocks?

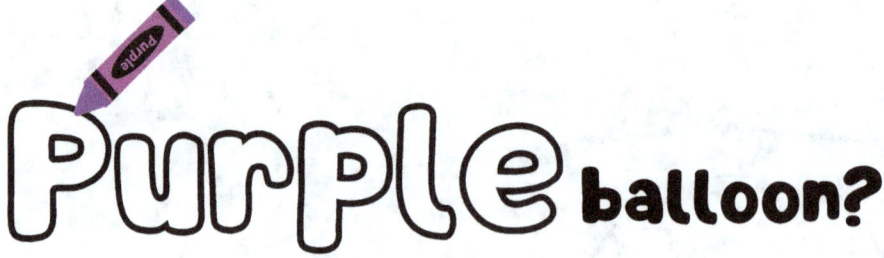

Purple balloon?

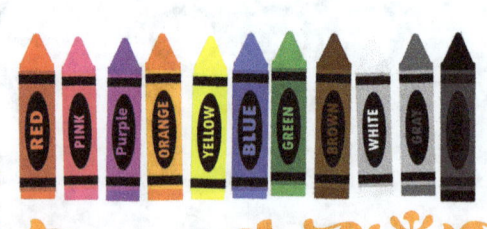

Toys

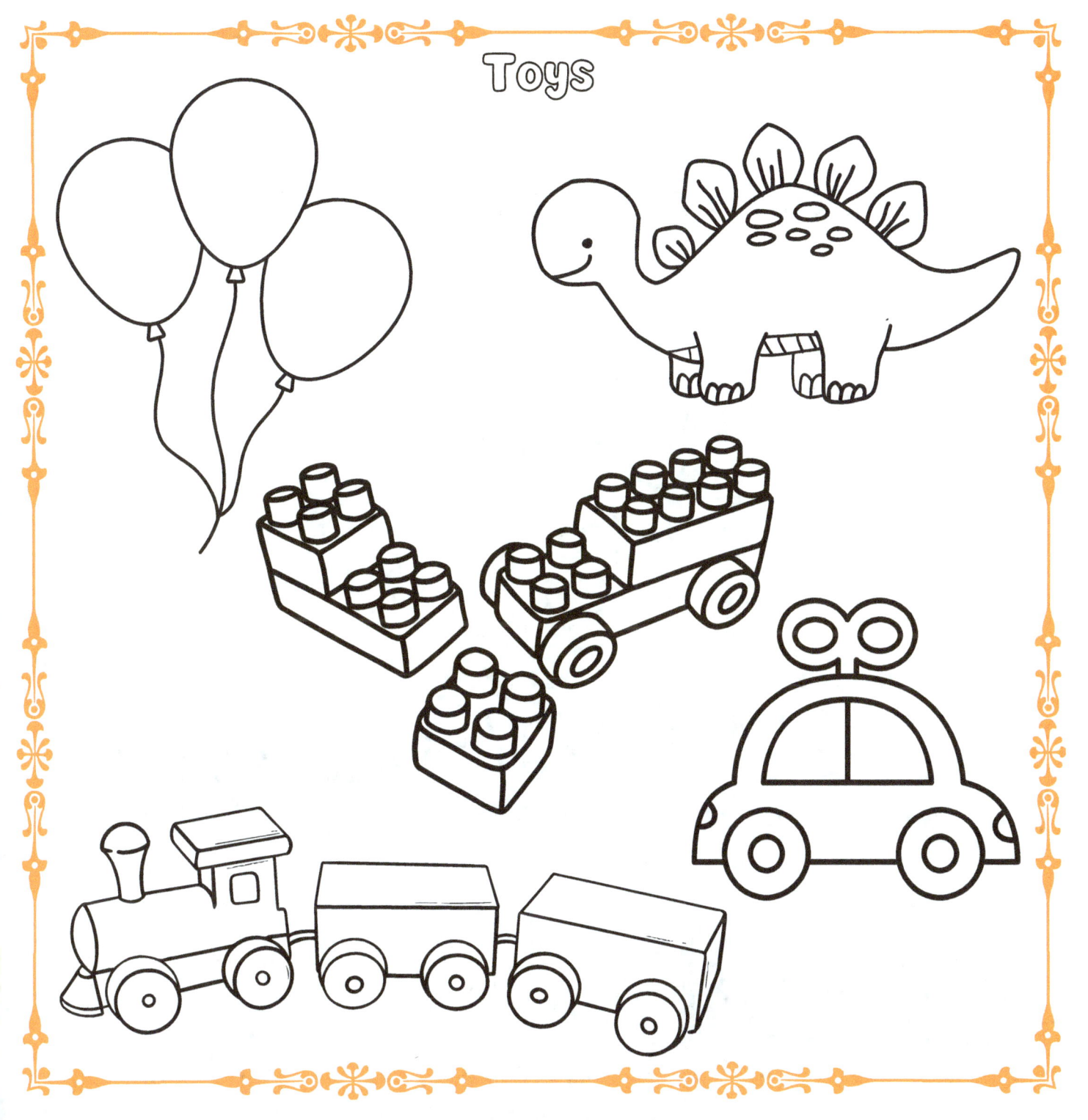

What colors can you find?

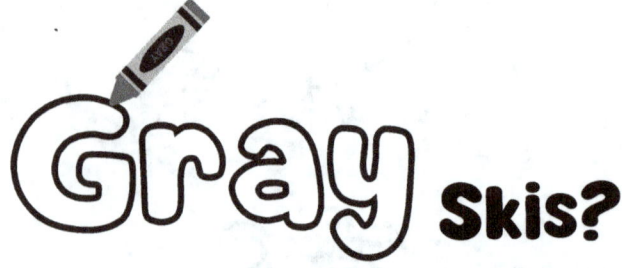 **Gray** Skis?

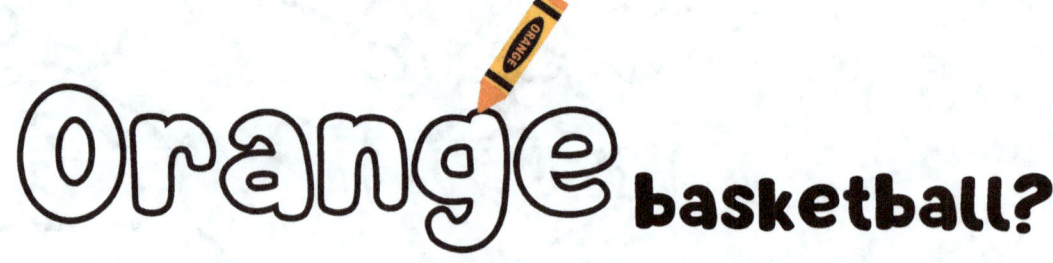 **Orange** basketball?

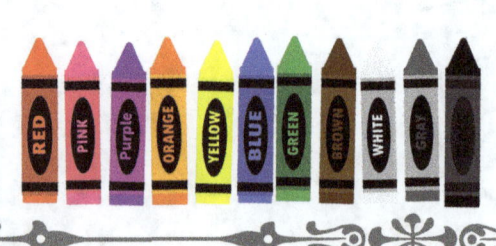

sports

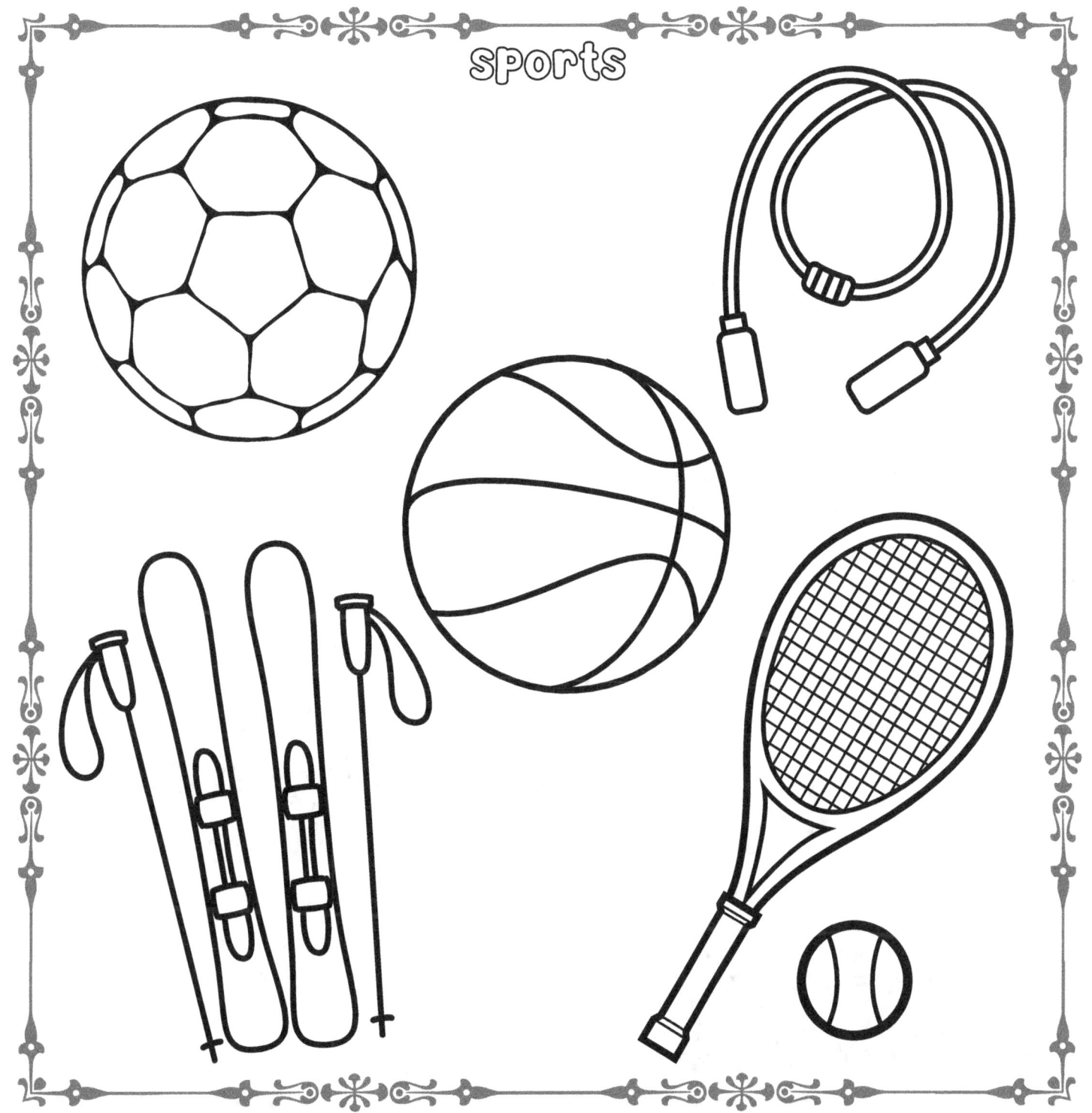

What colors can you find?

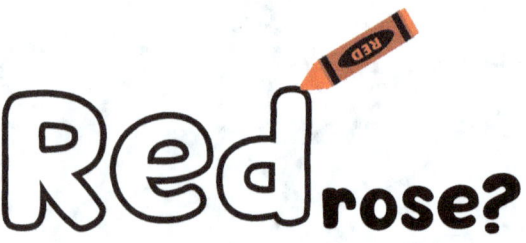

Red rose?

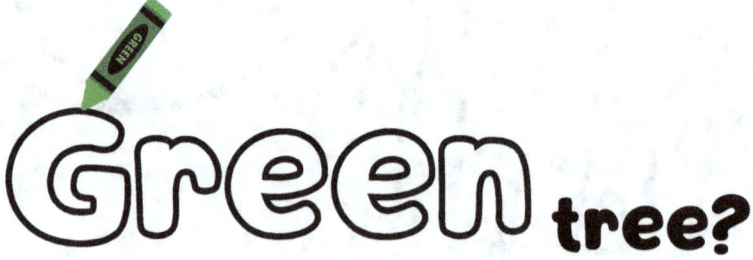

Green tree?

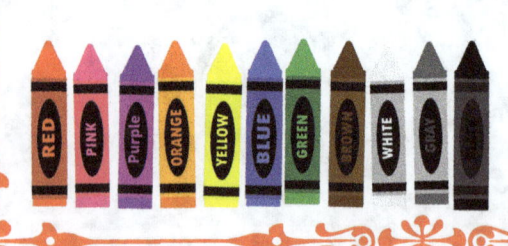

Plants

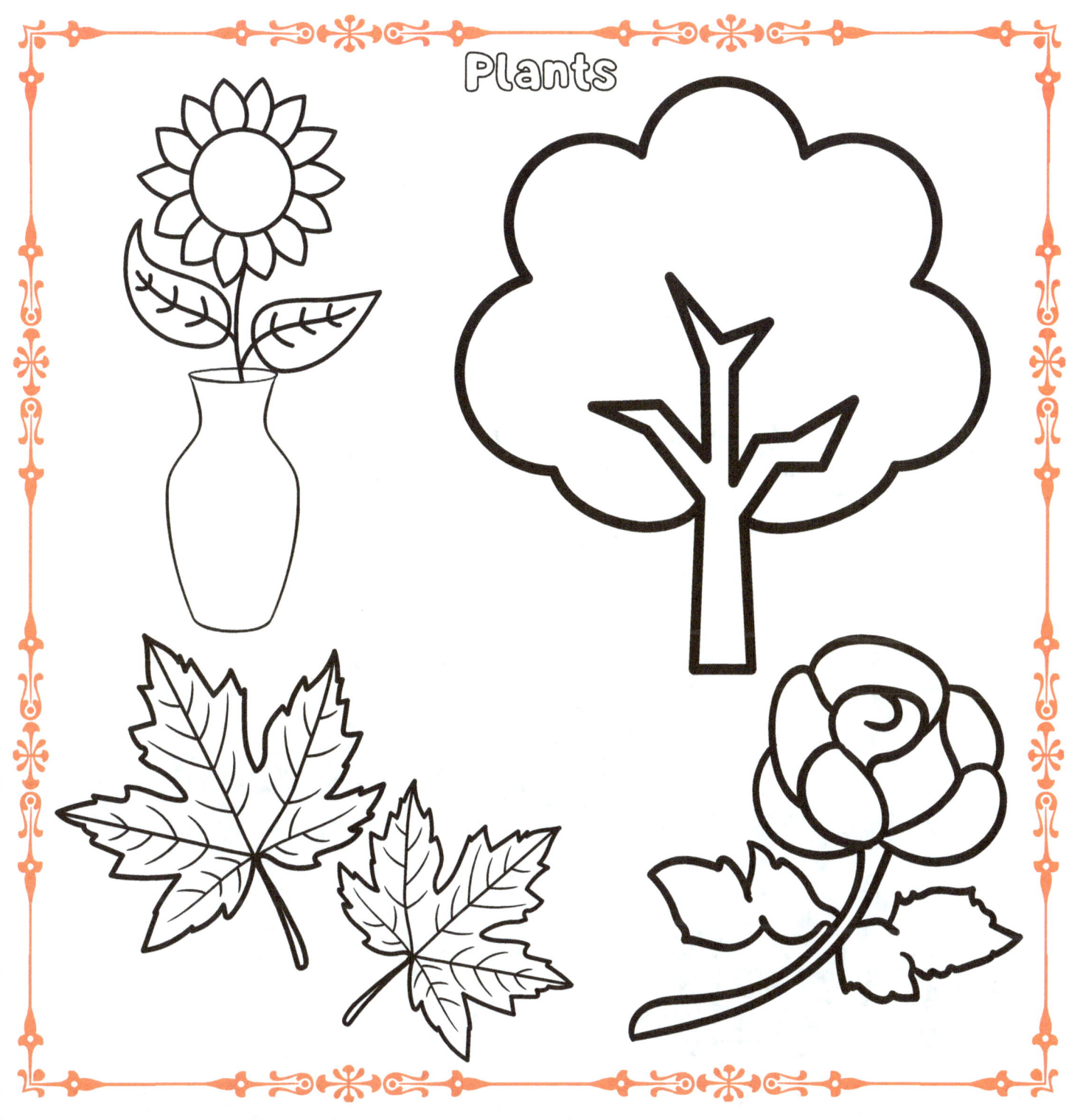

What colors can you find?

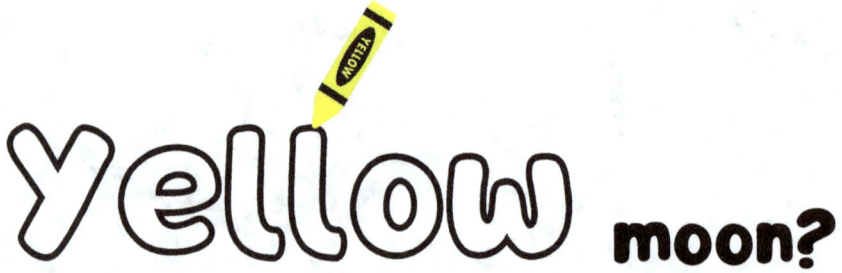 **Yellow** moon?

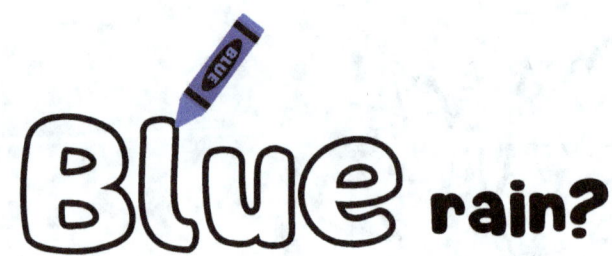 **Blue** rain?

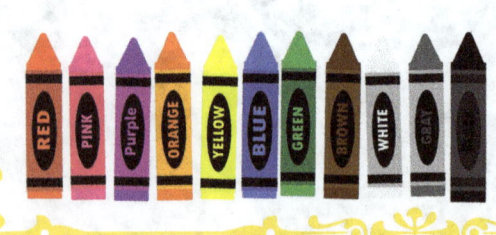

Sky

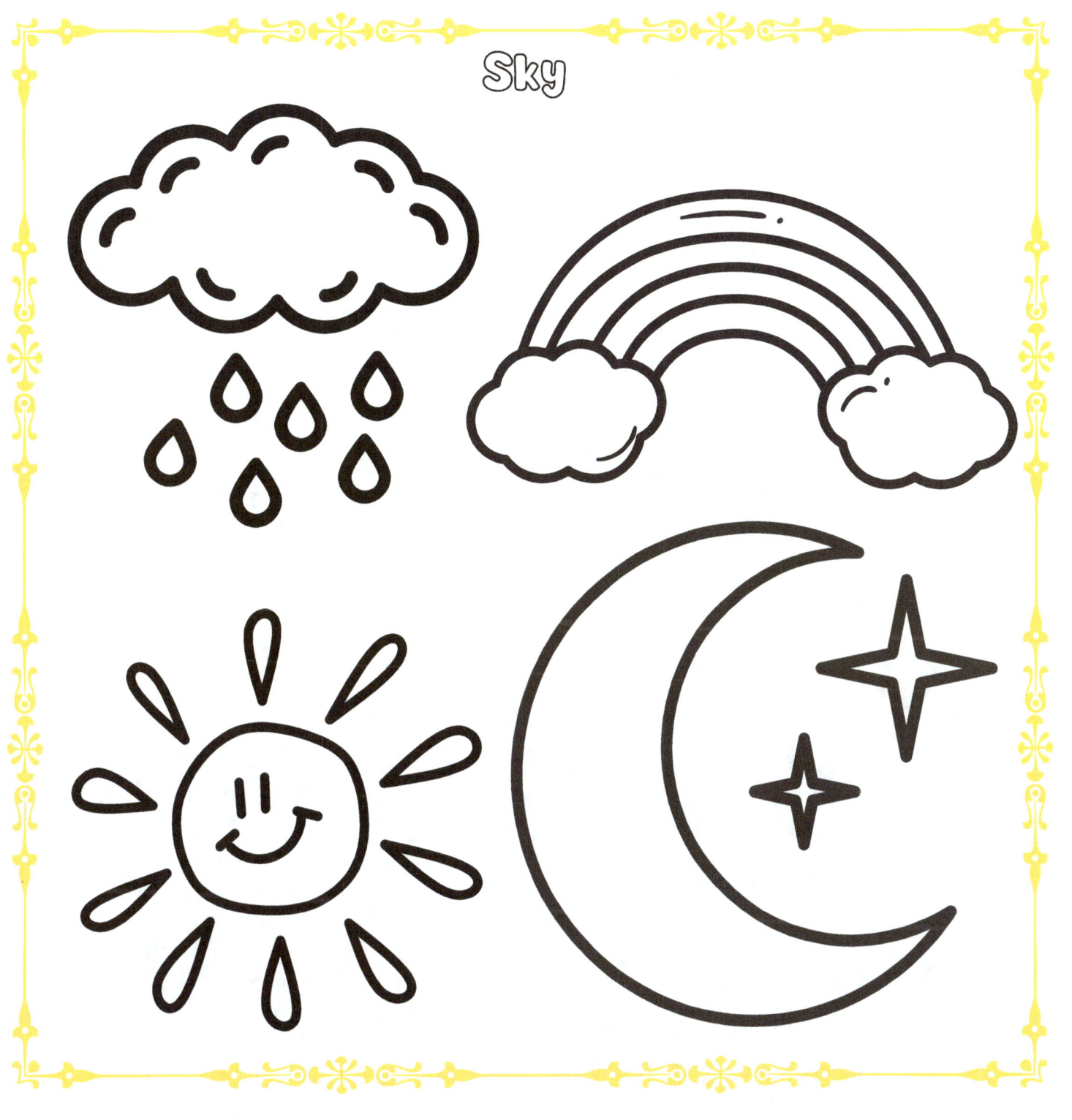

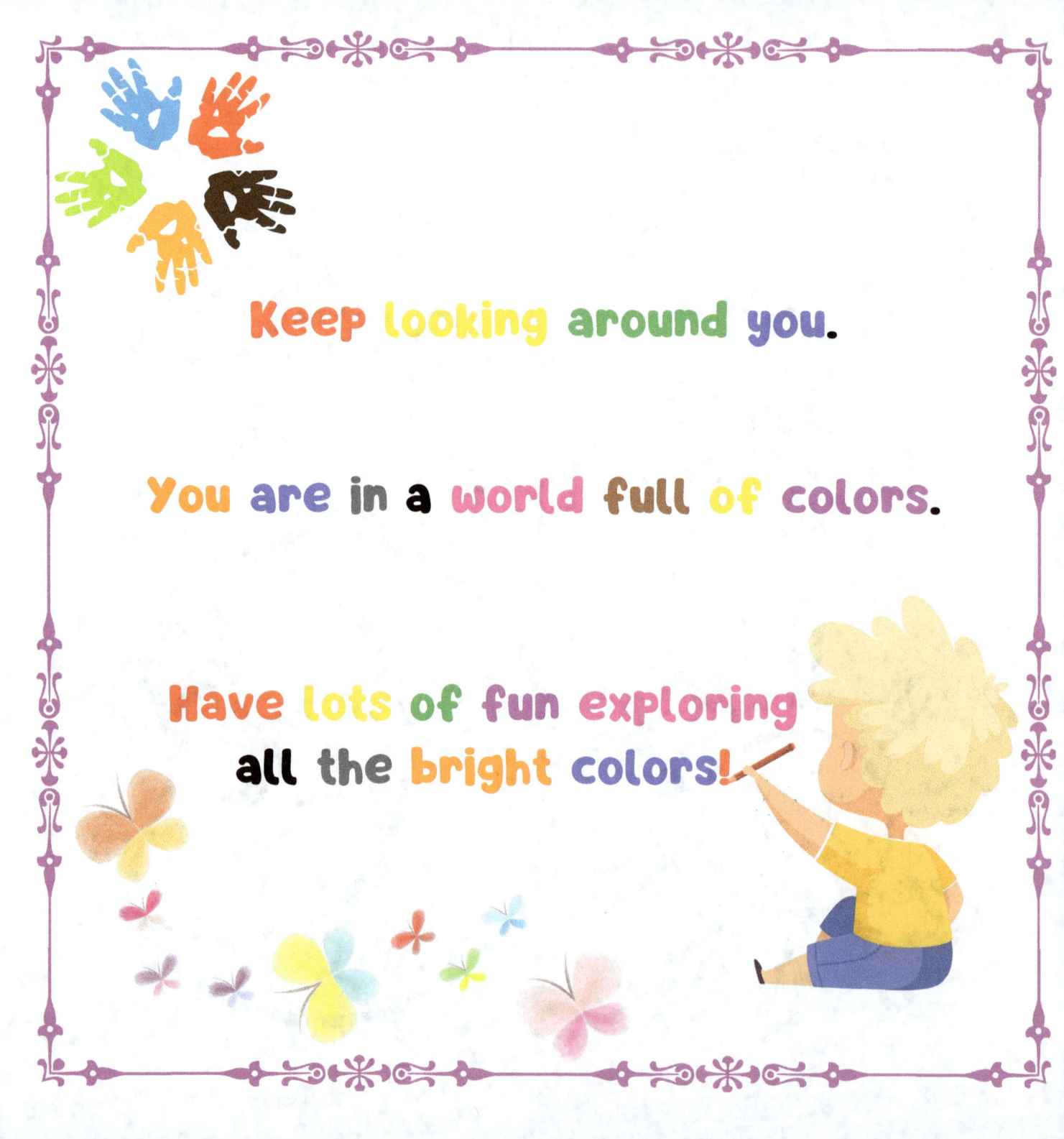

Keep looking around you.

You are in a world full of colors.

Have lots of fun exploring
all the bright colors!

www.ingramcontent.com/pod-product-compliance
Lightning Source LLC
Chambersburg PA
CBHW082148290526
45794CB00008B/3206